FROM BELLEAU WOOD TO BOUGAINVILLE

**The Oral History of Major General Robert Blake USMC
and The Travel Journal of Rosselet Wallace Blake**

by

Robert Wallace Blake

authorHOUSE

1663 LIBERTY DRIVE, SUITE 200
BLOOMINGTON, INDIANA 47403
(800) 839-8640
www.authorhouse.com

First published by AuthorHouse 10/08/04

ISBN: 1-4184-1155-8 (e)
ISBN: 1-4184-1156-6 (sc)

Printed in the United States of America
Bloomington, Indiana

This book is printed on acid-free paper.

For Rosselet and Robert Blake

Table of Contents

Part I

The Oral History

Interview

Family background. Mare Island and Quantico. Pontanezen, 17th
Company at Belleau Wood and Soissons. Hospital. 66th Company at
Meuse-Argonne. Charlie Barrett, Roy Hunt, Sam Cummings, George
Hamilton, William Matthews. Generals Harbord, Lejeune, Neville.
Armistice day action. Occupation duty at Niederbreitbach. Parades in New
York and Washington.

Quantico. Generals Butler and Puller. Russell and Neville Boards.
Orient cruise with SECNAV (*USS Henderson*). Pacific Fleet in USS
Pennsylvania, Mare Island and Goat Island. Nicaragua hill duty. Marine
Corps Schools. Nicaragua election duty. Spanish language mission in
Madrid and Salamanca.

Nicaraguan Electoral Commission. Marine Corps School faculty
with General Breckenridge: Charlie Barrett, Pete del Valle, DeWitt Peck.
Showing the flag in Latin-America. ONI Latin-America desk. Naval War
College. CO of Fifth Marines. Admiral Kimmel. Generals Geiger, Torrey ,
and Vandegrift.

Part II

The Travel Journal of Rosselet Wallace Blake

Acknowledgments

I wish to express my thanks:

To the Marine Corps Historical Center for making available my father's Oral History Transcript.

To Benis Frank and Jon Hoffman for their encouragement and assistance.

To Carol Beaupre for her elegant re-transcription of the original document.

To Polly and Fred Linhoss of TypeRight for their careful typescript of my mother's handwritten jouranl.

To Steven Sanford for transmitting the illustrations to the publisher via his computer.

To the USMC Personal Papers Collection for the use of the photos on pages 65-71.

Introduction

The main portion of this book consists of the Oral History of Major General Robert Blake USMC, as told to Marine historian Benis Frank. In 1972 the Marine Corps Historical Center bound two copies of the interview transcript, and recently reproduced it electronically. The transcript is published here verbatim from an electronic copy of the original, furnished by the Historical Center.

The second part of this book, the journal of Rosselet Wallace Blake, has not previously been published.

In 1918 my father, then a 1st lieutenant, won the first of his two Navy Crosses for his role with the 5th Marines at Belleau Wood in World War I. In 1943, as a colonel, he was awarded the Legion of Merit for his role in the landing at Bougainville by the 3rd Marine Division. Hence the title of this book.

My father, General Blake, retired in 1949 after thirty-two years service spanning both World Wars. In 1968 he was interviewed at his home in Oakland by Benis Frank, head of the USMC Oral History program. Present during the interview was my stepmother, Elynor Alexander Blake. She was the "third person in the room" noted at one point in the interview. As she had not known my father until after World War II, she was very interested in the events of his career before they had met. Though she did not know it, she had only a few more months to live. My father was then 74 and lived another fifteen years.

He died in 1983. That is when I first read his Oral History interview. Like most such interviews, this one focused on the military career itself, as opposed to life in the military. Several of my father's peacetime assignments were passed over lightly, including our family years in Spain and Panama, which figured large in my own life. Spanish history and literature also became my father's avocation. He collected a small library in Spanish that filled the shelves of a large reading room on the third floor of his and Elynor's house on Divisidero Street in San Francisco.

With the help of Benis Frank for records of my father's military career, and a probe of family documents and my own memories, I pieced together a narrative of my father's life which I originally saw as a companion to the Oral History. That is not what happened, but my memoir was eventually published in 2002 as *Bayonets and Bougainvilleas* by 1st Books Library.

Since then I have heard from a number of readers of that book. Many of them observed that I had made frequent references to my father's Oral History, but nowhere had I reported its contents. Others asked why I had not said more about my mother, since she had seemed very important in my life with my father away so much. So here they both are, in their own words; my father with Benis Frank, and my mother in her journal.

My father's Oral History ends with his retirement. My mother's journal begins in Quantico and ends with World War II, which she did not survive. My father's early life is capsuled in the Oral History. In a preface to my mother's journal I have given a brief account of her early years. For more than that, a reader must refer to *Bayonets and Bougainvilleas*.

Robert Wallace Blake
Seattle 2004

Part I

The Oral History

Robert Wallace Blake

Foreword

This typescript, the transcribed memoir of Major General Robert Blake, USMC (Retired) results from a tape-recorded interview conducted with him at his home in Oakland, California on 28 March 1968 for the Marine Corps Oral History Program. As one facet of the Marine Corps historical collection effort, this program obtains, by means of tape-recorded interviews, primary source material to augment documentary evidence.

Oral History is essentially spoken history, the oral recall of eyewitness impressions and observations recorded accurately on tape in the course of an interview conducted by an historian or an individual employing historical methodology and possibly the techniques of a journalist. The final product is a verbatim transcript containing historically valuable personal narratives relating to noteworthy professional experiences and observations from active duty, reserve, and retired distinguished Marines.

General Blake has read the transcript and made only minor corrections and emendations. The reader is asked to bear in mind, therefore, that he is reading a transcript of the spoken rather than the written word. General Blake has placed a restriction of PERMISSION REQUIRED TO CITE OR QUOTE on the use of both his interview tapes and transcripts. This means that a potential user is required to obtain permission in writing from General Blake or his heirs before quoting or citing from either the transcript or the recording.

Copies of this memoir are deposited in the Marine Corps Oral History Collection, Historical Division, Headquarters, U. S. Marine Corps, Washington, D. C.; Special Collections, Butler Library, Columbia University, New York, N. Y.; Oral History Collection, United States Naval Institute, Annapolis, Maryland; and the Manuscript Collection, Breckinridge Library, Marine Corps Development and Education Command, Quantico, Virginia.

E. H. Simmons
Brigadier General, U. S. Marine Corps (Retired)
Director of Marine Corps History and Museums

Signed:
30 October 1973

Brigadier General Blake as Inspector General of the Marine Corps, 1946.
USMC Photo

Robert Wallace Blake

Biographical Sketch – Major General Robert Blake

Major General Robert Blake, USMC, (Retired), was Chief of Staff of the 3rd Marine Division during the Empress Augusta Bay operations on Bougainville, and Deputy Island Commander, Guam, Mariana Islands, during World War II.

For outstanding services in these capacities he was awarded a Legion of Merit and a Gold Star in lieu of a second Legion of Merit. His citation for the former reads in part, "Colonel Blake capably coordinated the work of the executive and special staffs in planning and executing the difficult amphibious operations."

"He consulted with and advised the Commanding General and officers of all other units, with relation to the numerous details involved in the solution of problems of logistics."

"He was responsible for the coordination of air and naval support, and the strategic planning for an attack conducted under the most adverse conditions, resulting from tropical climate and enemy opposition."

"His sound judgment and professional skill contributed materially to the success of the campaign."

General Blake was born on 17 August 1894, in Seattle, Washington. After graduating from the University of California he reported for active duty on 19 May 1917, as a second lieutenant in the Marine Corps.

He sailed for France in October 1917, and as a member of the 5th Marine Regiment participated in the defense of the Verdun Sector, the Aisne-Marne Defensive (Chateau-Thierry), the Aisne-Marne Offensive (Soissons), the St. Mihiel Offensive and the Meuse-Argonne Offensive. He was a member of the Army of Occupation in Germany until July 1919, when he sailed for the United States.

The General was awarded the Navy Cross for extraordinary heroism in action near Belleau Wood on 6 June 1918. His citation reads in part, "When the line was temporarily held up, he volunteered and maintained liaison with the 49th Company, continually crossing and recrossing an open field swept by intense machine-gun fire."

In addition to the Navy Cross he received the Distinguished Service Cross, the Silver Star, the French Croix de Guerre with Gilt Star and Bronze Star, and the Belgian Ordre de la Couronne with rank of Chevalier. He is entitled to wear the French Fourragere.

From January 1920 to April 1922, the General was successively a student and an instructor at the Marine Officers' Infantry School, Quantico, Virginia. In June 1922, he became Commanding Officer of the Marine Detachment on board the

USS *Henderson* and Aide-de-Camp to the Secretary of the Navy on a cruise to Japan for a period of about four months.

In September 1922, he went to duty at the Marine Barracks, Mare Island, California, where he remained until June 1923, when he went to sea duty as Commanding Officer, Marine Detachment, USS *Pennsylvania*. Upon detachment he was assigned as Commanding Officer, Marine Detachment, Receiving Ship at San Francisco, where he remained for two years until ordered to foreign shore duty in January 1928.

He served with the 11th Regiment of the 2nd Marine Brigade in Nicaragua as Commanding Officer of the 2nd Battalion and was awarded a Gold Star in lieu of a second Navy Cross for action against insurrectionists.

Upon return to the United States in September 1929, he was assigned as a student at the Field Officers' Course, Marine Corps Schools, and upon graduation he returned to Nicaragua with the Electoral Mission.

In March 1931 he was ordered to Madrid, Spain, for one year of duty and instruction in Spanish. Upon completion he returned to the Nicaragua Electoral Mission.

In December 1932, the General joined the staff of the Marine Corps Schools, Quantico, Virginia, as an instructor in the Field Officers' Course. In June 1934, he became Chief of the One and Two Sections of the Schools.

He went to sea duty in June 1935, as Squadron Marine Officer aboard the USS *Trenton* and the USS *Memphis*.

From September 1937 to June 1940 he was on duty in the Office of Naval Intelligence, Navy Department, Washington, D.C., during which period he served on temporary duty as a member of a Good Will cruise to South America.

Following duty in Washington, the General was assigned as a student in the Senior Course, Naval War College, Newport, Rhode Island, and upon graduation was ordered to the 1st Marine Division where he took command of the 5th Marines. He held that position when the United States entered World War II.

In June 1942, he took command of the 10th Defense Battalion and led this battalion into action on the Russell Islands, Southern Solomons, and provided the antiaircraft defense of that island. In addition he was Commander, Marine Defense Groups, Solomons, from June to August 1943.

He next became Chief of Staff of the 3rd Marine Division which position he held until taking command of the 21st Marines of the division in February 1944.

Upon the invasion of Guam in July 1944, he was Chief of Staff of the Island Command and in March of the following year became Deputy Island Commander.

In June 1945, he was assigned, as Marine Deputy Chief of Staff, Tenth Army on Okinawa, and in November 1945, became Commanding General of the Occupation Forces, Truk and Central Caroline Islands.

The General returned to the United States in June 1946, and was named President of the Post War Personnel Reorganization Board at Headquarters Marine Corps in Washington, D.C. On 1 October 1946, he assumed duty as Inspector General, Marine Corps, in which capacity he was serving when he was retired on 30 June 1949. He was advanced to his present rank on the retired list at that time for having been specially commended for the performance of duty in actual combat.

In addition to the Navy Cross with Gold Star, Distinguished Service Cross, Silver Star, French Croix de Guerre with Gilt Star and Bronze Star, and the Belgian Ordre de la Couronne with rank of Chevalier, his decorations and medals include the Legion of Merit; Gold Star in lieu of a second Legion of Merit; Victory Medal with Aisne, Aisne-Marne, St. Mihiel, Meuse-Argonne and Defensive Sector Clasps; Army of Occupation of Germany Medal; Second Nicaraguan Campaign Medal; American Defense Service Medal with Bronze Star; American Campaign Medal; Asiatic-Pacific Campaign Medal with four Bronze Stars; World War II Victory Medal; Nicaraguan Medal of Merit with Silver Star; Abdon Calderon Star First Class (Ecuador); and the French Fourragere.

Interview

Interview with Major General Robert Blake, USMC (Retired), conducted by Mr. Benis M. Frank, Head, Oral History Unit, Historical Branch, G-3 Division, Headquarters Marine Corps, on 27 March 1968 at the General's home in Oakland, California. This interview consists of two reels recorded at 1-78 ips

<u>World War I 1917-19</u>

Frank: The first thing I generally ask, General, of the people I interview is how they happened to join the Marine Corps. Now, you were born in Seattle, so you're a west coast native, and then you went to the University of California. Was there anyone who had been in military life from your family?

Blake: No, except my father had several brothers in the Civil War; and my mother's grandfather had served in the British Navy during the Napoleonic wars.

Frank: Had you any knowledge of his history or records?

Blake: Just what Mother told me.

Frank: Your mother was English born then?

Blake: Canadian.

Frank: Was your father a professional man?

Blake: No, he was general superintendent of the Pacific coast division of the Postal Telegraph Company, now defunct, at the time I entered the Marine Corps. He was a Vermonter.

Frank: Oh, good New England stock then. Well, now, you came into the Marine Corps in 1917 just shortly after we entered the war. Had you known anything about the Marine Corps before this?

Blake: Very little.

Frank: How did you happen to choose the Marine Corps?

Blake: Well, quite frankly it was because I was able to get a commission without having to go through the Army training camp. Quite a number of commissions were available for alumni from the University of California who had completed their military work at the University satisfactorily. I didn't particularly like the thought of going into the Army, and the Marine Corps seemed more interesting.

Frank: Who else joined with you at this time who made any record or who remained in the Marine Corps?

Blake:	Oliver Smith, General Hermle, and General Brooks. It's so long ago it's hard to think of them offhand.
Frank:	They were all in the same class at the University of California. They all came in from California.
Blake:	Yes, those that came in primarily from the '15, '16, '17 class at that time.
Frank:	You went immediately to the officers' training class.
Blake:	We reported at Mare Island. I reported at Mare Island – I think it was in May 1917 – and we were there until July, when we were sent to the officers' training school at Marine Barracks, Quantico, Virginia, which at that time was just a red mud slashing out of the Virginia hillside.
Frank:	What did you do at Mare Island for two months?
Blake:	Drilled, shot on the range, got indoctrinated.
Frank:	All the lieutenants were formed up into a platoon and drilled by an NCO or something. Or did they have an officer drilling then?
Blake:	An officer.
Frank:	Which officers' training class was this that you attended at Quantico?
Blake:	The first one.
Frank:	Do you remember some of the people that were in there?
Blake:	General Hill, General Worton; General Smith went to Guam – he didn't go to Quantico. It's hard to remember the names offhand.
Frank:	Yes, Well, it might develop as we go on. What was the training class like?
Blake:	It was very primitive, principally boot camp drill. We had some class work. We did some mapping, but it was nothing like they get now. I remember General Barrett saying later that he received a letter of commendation for the work that he did in those officers' training schools. He said: "I should have gotten a general court martial." Of course it wasn't his fault. It wasn't anybody's fault. They just didn't know.
Frank:	Oh, really? Did you get to know Barrett?
Blake:	Yes.
Frank:	When was that?
Blake:	Throughout my Marine Corps life. He had one of the companies at Quantico.
Frank:	Oh, this is Charlie Barrett.
Blake:	Yes.
Frank:	Yes, Charlie Barrett came in a little earlier.
Blake:	Yes, he was a captain then; and Captain Lee was in charge of the student officer company that I was in.
Frank:	Was this Harry Lee?

Blake: No. He was known as "Mandy" Lee – a very nice person.

Frank: You remained there until you left for France.

Blake: France. Let me see: we sailed from Philadelphia on the *Von Steuben* the latter part of October, 1917 – the first convoy into Brest.

Frank: What outfit were you assigned to in the 5th Marines? Were you in a battalion?

Blake: I think there were 11 of us who went over as casuals with the battalion of the 6th Marines that was embarked on the *Von Steuben* to join the 5th Regiment. I got sidetracked at Brest and was there until the middle of January 1918, when I managed to get ordered to the regiment.

Frank: What were you doing in Brest?

Blake: I was assistant to the base adjutant.

Frank: Was that an Army or a Marine Corps function?

Blake: Army. Colonel, later Major General Bash, or a name very similar was the base commander.

Frank: It must have been pretty much of a mess there at this time, wasn't it?

Blake: It hadn't started to become a mess yet, because the great mass of troops hadn't begun yet to pour through Brest.

Frank: Was anything organized to any great degree?

Blake: Well, there was quite a bit of cargo coming through, and such troops that came through, as I remember, went to the French barracks at the outskirts of Brest, at Pontanezen.

Frank: Smedley Butler hadn't come over yet, had he?

Blake: Oh, no.

Frank: Was Pontanezen pretty much of a mess?

Blake: Not then. It was sort of a quaint old place in the charming Brittany countryside.

Frank: How were you able to get yourself detached and sent back to the 5th Marines?

Blake: Well, an order came out from headquarters AEF directing that all personnel on detached duty belonging to certain divisions be returned to their organizations. And Colonel Bash kindly interpreted that as applying to me, although I'd never actually joined the 5th Regiment.

Frank: Well, for record purposes, you joined or rejoined the 5th Regiment in January.

Blake   I joined it for the first time in January 1918. You see, I'd never actually reported to it before. I was not on its rolls.

Frank: They were where at that time?

Blake: They were in the training area in the Haute Marne. The battalion to which I was assigned was at Breuvannes.

Frank: Were you assigned to a battalion immediately?

12

Blake: Yes, the 17th Company, 1st Battalion, 5th Marines.

Frank: Who had it at that time?

Blake: General Hunt – Captain Hunt.

Frank: And the battalion commander was . . .?

Blake: I forget his name. He was relieved before we went into action, and Major Turrill commanded the battalion.

Frank: It wasn't Berry or Hughes, was it?

Blake: No, Hughes was in the 6th. This was Turrill. He was retired as a colonel.

Frank: What was the battalion doing at this time?

Blake: Training.

Frank: What type of training?

Blake: Training for combat.

Frank: Strictly trench warfare?

Blake: Yes.

Frank: Bayonets and so on?

Blake: Yes.

Frank: Was it conducting its own training or were the French supervising it?

Blake: At that time there were no French instructors with the regiment. There had been. They'd gotten along very nicely. The Marines always seemed to get on well with foreigners. As a matter of fact, there was an article at the time published in an American magazine – I remember reading it – in which it said how much better the Marines seemed to get along with the French than the Army did.

Frank: What was the first action you went into?

Blake: Belleau Woods on Hill 142.

Frank: The 5th Marines was on the right at that time, was it not – on the right of Meaux Highway.

Blake: Well, the 1st Battalion . . . We knew very little about what was going on. I think in the last action, on the 1st of November when we attacked, the privates knew more about what was going on than the company commanders did and certainly more than the platoon commanders did at Belleau Wood. I never saw any written orders nor had a map nor received anything but the sketchiest of oral orders. The situation was changing too fast. I know now that we were about two miles north of the present Chateau Thierry – La Ferte – Meaux highway; that would be on the left side of the highway going toward Chateau Thierry. We just walked through a wood, over the crest of a ridge, down the far side to the edge of the wood where I ran into a Gunnery Sergeant, Sid Thayer who later was commissioned, who said the Germans were across the field to the front. We relieved no one. We saw only two French soldiers wandering to the rear. We were on the left flank of the 2nd Division with no one visible on our left. I remember receiving little or no hostile fire until the company was withdrawn from that position to attack down (north) Hill 142 as reserve company. Captain Winans had been called to Battalion Headquarters and left me with instructions to follow with the company as soon as we were relieved by the French. They were late in arriving. When we crossed the ridge moving to the rear, we passed through heavy light artillery fire. As well as I can remember, casualties were light. I received a very slight nick from a tiny shell fragment that penetrated the leather facing on the inside of one leg of the British artillery trousers I was wearing. I remember no preparatory bombardment nor supporting concentrations from our artillery. After the war, when talking with an officer from the 15th Field Artillery, I asked why. He said that his battery had no orders to support the attack and that he knew nothing about it until it was over. By the time we had reach the line of departure, the assault waves had disappeared down the ridge into a wood. The 17th Company following through the wood and deployed on the far side under heavy small arms fire from the left. Bert Baston, All-American tackle from the University of Minnesota, was seriously wounded in the leg here. I slipped over the ridge to the right and found a ravine, extending north and south, toward the front, filled with German dead. I returned to Company Headquarters and asked Captain Winans if I could have two men to go with me to see if I could locate the assault waves. He concurred. We dropped down into the ravine, proceeded forward some distance, then crept up the slope through the brush and found the remains of the assault companies, 48th and 66th, Captain George Hamilton in command, deployed across the ridge at the rear edge of another wood, presumably on the objective. The field to the rear was under the same heavy fire that the 17th company was being subjected to. A company of Marines that proved to be, I believe, the 52nd Company, Second Battalion, was trying to work across it. I told Captain Hamilton that I could bring the 17th Company up to join him without any losses, which I did. After that, so as Captain Hamilton and Captain Winans were concerned, I could do no wrong. The 17th Company moved into the front line on the left flank. Later that day a platoon of the 52nd Company under, I believe, First Lieutenant, now Major General, Retired, Samuel C. Cumming, established a line across the gully on our left presumably to make contact with the French who were slowly moving down a ridge parallel to Hill 142. Some time later, the 17th Company relieved that platoon when the 52nd Company was relieved to participate, I presume, in an attack on our right flank in Belleau Wood proper.

Frank: You had a platoon at this time?

Blake: Well, I was executive officer of the company. Captain Winans had relieved Captain Hunt.

Frank: That's Roswell Winans?

Blake: Roswell Winans, yes. I was sent to the platoon leaders' school at Gondrecourt in March 1918 for six weeks while the regiment was training for trench warfare in a quiet sector of the Verdun front. A few days after my return, we entrucked for an unannounced sector of the front in connection with the German breakthrough that had occurred in March. We ended up in the Chateau Thierry area.

Frank: How would you characterize the fighting that your company saw at Belleau Wood?

Blake: It was difficult. The casualties were heavy.

Frank: Was there much competition between the 5th Regiment and the 6th Regiment?

Blake: Not particularly. I wouldn't say there was any rivalry. Of course everybody thought their own regiment was the better.

Frank: You were part of the 4th Brigade at this time of the 2nd Division.

Blake: That's right.

Frank: Had Lejeune come over yet?

Blake: I don't believe that General Lejeune came over until after Belleau Wood. You see, General Harboard commanded the brigade then; and the story was (and this may be purely apocryphal) that General Pershing gave him the brigade because he wanted to make him a major general, and the 4th Brigade of the Marines would give him the assurance of making a record that would justify his promotion. After that he was promoted and had the division. I'm sure General Harboard had the division at Soissons. Colonel Neville was promoted and took the brigade.

Frank: Do you recall what the relationship on, say, the company level of the brigade as a whole was with the Army; how it felt about being within an Army division?

Blake: Well, we didn't like being part of the Army, but I think we accepted it as a matter of fact. I think by and large we liked it better when the division was attached to the French for an operation.

Frank: What operation was that for?

Blake: Soissons and the Champagne and perhaps Belleau Wood – I don't know. Everything was so confused at that time. But I believe that the 2nd Division was operationally under the control of the French for

Belleau Wood (Aisne-Marne Defensive), the Soissons attack (Aisne-Marne Offensive) and Blanc Mont Ridge in the Champagne (Meuse-Argonne Offensive). It was under American operational control for the St. Mihiel offensive and for the attack 1-11 November, also included under the term Meuse Argonne offensive.

Frank: When you returned from the officers' school at Gondrecourt you immediately went back into the lines for the Chateau Thierry. Was that different in any sense so far as terrain was concerned in relation to Belleau Wood? Was the nature of the operations different?

Blake: Well, Chateau Thierry was the general term used for that entire operation.

Frank: The Aisne-Marne.

Blake: Yes, the Aisne-Marne. What did they call it? - defensive. We never saw Chateau Thierry, as a matter of fact. And how far Belleau Wood and Hill 142 are from Chateau Thierry, I don't know.

Frank: Immediately after that you went into the Aisne-Marne offensive at Soissons.

Blake: Yes.

Frank: That was pretty much the same type of fighting?

Blake: Well, it was different in this respect: it was more organized; we had more artillery; it was a huge general offensive – whereas Belleau Wood and 142 seemed more of a small unit action. The terrain was flatter at Soissons. We attacked through woods and soon got out into the open fields, and it was largely a question of following the barrage.

Frank: Would you say after the first baptism of fire, Belleau Wood, which probably was about the first for the 5th Regiment, that the regiment remained as aggressive and as offensively minded or a little bit more cautious?

Blake: I saw no difference.

Frank: It retained its offensive spirit?

Blake: Oh, yes. Of course, when you're tired and hungry and exhausted, you don't think much of those things. The French troops were really nonexistent at Belleau Wood.

Frank: They weren't at that time. Did the regiment take a high proportion of casualties?

Blake: It did in Belleau Wood, not so heavy at Soissons. As I say, it was a better-organized attack. The Germans were caught completely by surprise. When the 1st Battalion hit them, they were down in their dugouts eating breakfast.

Frank: The replacement system worked readily? In other words, the ranks were filled almost as soon as they were depleted?

Blake: Oh, yes, we got replacements for Soissons just before we took off from where we were billeted down in the Marne – I forget the name of the village. That was a surprisingly secret operation. When the trucks came for us we thought we were going to St. Denis, or some other village near Paris for rest and recreation. How they did it is beyond my comprehension, and how they got that vast force together . . .

Frank: This is for Soissons.

Blake: Yes. It was really something – that march to the front. During the heavy rain and windstorm, the night of the 17th and 18th, the highway was packed with artillery. I bumped my head into the rear end of more horses than I thought existed, because you couldn't see your hand in front of your face. And going down that road in single file, weaving through the artillery down in the ditch on one side, and then across the road and down into the ditch on the other with lightning flashing and thunder crashing – I don't know how the battalion ever got there.

Frank: But it did intact.

Blake: Intact absolutely. Right on time. The only way we got our extra bandoliers of ammunition was that we happened to go by a dump that I believe had been left for the 1st Division. The day broke clear, we scooped up our extra bandoliers of ammunition, went down the road to the jump-off point. Captain Hunt was back with the battalion then, commanding 17th Company. I remember Major Turrill calling him back to give him instructions. He told me to go ahead with the company and deploy it and take off, which we did. We were the left flank company of the division hooked up with the French Moroccan division. That particular unit was Senegalese troops – big, black, scar-faced panthers. They fired their chauchat from the shoulder. They handled that chauchat gun as if it were a toy.

Frank: Did they prefer the knife rather than . . .?

Blake: No, I never saw them use a knife. Some of our men nearly got into fights with them, because they wanted to kill prisoners that had surrendered. I remember vividly one of my automatic riflemen grabbing his chauchat gun by the muzzle and swinging it around his head and yelling at them: "Get back you black bastard."

Frank: I was going to ask you about the offensive spirit of the Germans. What were they like, the units you faced in this case?

Blake: Well, they surrendered very readily, but the Germans were always competent – highly competent.

Frank: Regardless of whether it was a crack outfit or . . .

Blake: Well, any that I experienced were highly competent.

Frank: It's very interesting that in World War I the company commanders had to go back to the battalion, and the battalion commanders had to go back to the regiment to get their orders rather than depending on communications of any type. This being the case, it generally fell to the executive officer – the battalion or company executive officer – to in many cases fight the unit.

Blake: Well, usually. Of course, the battalion was all together. Captain Hunt was back with us in a few minutes. We'd hardly reached the German lines when he was back.

Frank: One of the criticisms made about World War I – I think this applies perhaps more to the British than to the Americans, or at least maybe the British and the American Army and Marines – was the fact that the staff officers never came forward, never got their boots muddied. Was this the case with the Marines, or did you see, for instance, General Harboard up front and brigade staff up front and regimental staff up front?

Blake: Well, there wasn't any reason for them to be. If you mean by up front that relatively thin belt where anything that moves above ground gets shot at, I never saw any higher staff officers. I'd see no particular reason for them.

Frank: I was thinking in the case of the rudimentary communications that existed, depending purely on messengers . . .

Blake: And telephones.

Frank: And a basic telephone system. That was sufficient to keep, say, the rear . . .?

Blake: Informed of what was going on?

Frank: Yes.

Blake: That I don't know.

Frank: I was thinking of the criticism that's been made of, say, the British and perhaps of the American Army general staff remaining way in back, completely out of touch with the battle – as opposed to what we saw in World War II and even in Korea, where the regimental commanders and even the division commanders made personal reconnaissance, keeping tabs of what was going on.

Blake: Well, at the company level, to what extent that may be going on and the company officers not knowing about it, is difficult to say. It's a criticism that I wouldn't want to make, because it might be an unjust criticism.

Frank: I wasn't looking for criticisms so much as to determine what type of real control the regiment or the brigade had over the conduct of the operation.

Blake: Well, once the battle is joined, the only way higher command has any control over it is through the committing of reserves.

Frank: Of course you've studied World War I operations, I'm sure, after the fact. Would you say that, based on your schooling and knowledge, World War operations that you were in followed a typical school pattern; that the staff and command SOPs were followed?

Blake: Insofar as they had them. I would say of World War I that the combat training at the platoon level simply did not compare with what obviously goes on in the Marine Corps today.

Frank: You went on from Soissons to St. Mihiel, which was just a continuation of the overall operation?

Blake: Oh, it was an entirely different front. St. Mihiel salient was a long way from Soissons. It's hard for me to picture that in my mind.

Frank: I should have brought a map. St. Mihiel, if I recall my history of the period – was this where the whole American AEF was put in? This was a particularly bad salient, and I think the French high command asked Pershing to commit . . .

Blake: That was the first operation of the American Army as a unit. St. Mihiel was an old salient; for years had been a very inactive salient; and I would rather imagine had been selected as the first test of strength of the American Army because it would be an easy operation. The Germans didn't really fight until they'd fallen back to a line across the base of the salient. I fell and badly wrenched my knee during that operation, so except for the first couple of days, I was out of it and didn't come back until right after the division had come out of Champagne.

Frank: You were in the hospital, I think, for a period of about two weeks; and then you went to the First Training Regiment near Tours or Blois. You got back, rejoined the regiment on the 21st of October, and took part in the Meuse-Argonne.

Blake: Yes. I remember I was down with a terrific cold. I envisioned myself as coming down with pneumonia after the first night in a wet hole in the ground. The division had been ordered back into the lines when I joined. We were up close enough so that I had to get in a hole. I woke up in the morning without the slightest indication that I had ever had any trouble. Spending the night in the mud cured my cold completely. We didn't know that the flu epidemic was going on.

Frank: Did it hit the regiment at all?

Blake: No.

Frank: That was very fortunate.

Blake: We were out in the open all the time.

Frank: Had you been aware of or heard of or had any knowledge of the mutiny in the French Army?

Blake: None. The first word that I got of that was from a friend from home whom I ran into around the 8th or 9th of November. He was then assigned to the 17th Field Artillery. He'd been with the ambulance corps before we got into the war when the French mutiny occurred, and he told me about it. I thought it was just one of his wild stories – he tended that way. So I didn't know anything about it until years later when it was published in American magazines.

An interesting event occurred around the middle of June 1918 that I believe is worth recording. The 17th Company had just been placed in battalion reserve in a wood near and south of Bois Belleau when Captain Winans sent for me and said that the Second Battalion had established a line on the north edge of that wood, and hooked around the northwest corner a short distance to cover the left flank facing a wheat field, but that Germans were sending patrols around that flank, through the wheat field, and into the woods behind the battalion lines, by night. The 17th Company was to cover the west flank of Belleau Wood and keep the Germans out. He told me to take a platoon down, locate the left flank of second battalion, and report back. For that mission a platoon seemed too cumbersome so he consented to my going with three men. I proceeded down into the woods, keeping about 100 yards inside to be sure not to overrun the Marine left flank and soon came to a ravine filled with German dead. Some distance beyond that we came to a fair sized clearing filled with stacks of cordwood. About halfway across that we came under heavy German fire from the far side of the clearing and a grinning German head poked up over a woodpile. There were evidently no Marines in the position indicated on the map so we withdrew without injuries and reported back to Captain Winans. He then proceeded down into the wood with the company. At the dead German ravine, he told me to take my platoon and find the left flank of the Second Battalion and connect up with it. Our information was that it was Captain Zane's company. A wood road, little more than a wide trail, ran east and west a short distance south of the clearing. There I came upon First Lieutenant William R. Matthews, Intelligence Officer of Second Battalion, and told him my mission as well as showed him the map with the Second Battalion hooked around the northwest corner of the Wood. He replied that they weren't there at all and never had been and marked where I would find the flank, perhaps a kilometer to the east. I proceeded there, found the flank and also that Captain Zane's company was not the left flank company but the second company from the left flank. I then proceeded back to report to Captain Winans, dropped off groups of about four men each some twenty-five yards apart until I reached a north south wood road that formed the east edge of the aforementioned clearing. The company was relieved, or rather the battalion was relieved, by an Army unit, a day or two later and we moved to a village on the Marne River for five or ten days rest before returning to the lines. In the meantime, the regiment had attacked again to clean out that corner of the wood Second Battalion had left open. Apparently what had happened was that the night following the original attack, the Germans found that portion of the wood unoccupied by Marines and moved a battalion of their own heavily reinforced with machine guns back in. It seemed apparent that, in the heat of combat, after disposing of the Germans in the aforementioned ravine, the battalion had lost direction and guided on the east-west road on which I had found Lieutenant Matthews until they came out in the open again on the northeast side of the bulge made by the northwest portion of the wood. The interesting part is that apparently Matthews, who was a very obstinate as well as brilliant officer, got into an argument with Lieutenant Colonel Wise as to where the left flank of the battalion was and Colonel Wise fired him. Matthews was right, Wise was wrong. He may have trusted his front line company commanders more than he did his intelligence officer, who was considerably their junior, I believe, and didn't go take a look himself. Matthews was sent to the First Battalion. He said he thought he was going to get a general court martial, where he turned in a brilliant performance at Blanc Mont Ridge where he was wounded. He was given an outstanding fitness report by Major Hamilton, which was returned by Regiment, in view of Wise's report, for correction in the belief that a mistake had been made, but Hamilton, I am told, stuck to his guns.

Matthews was a newspaperman and resigned his commission following the armistice but applied for a recommissioning under the Neville Board out of curiosity to see what would happen. He was turned down. But I am sure he would not have accepted reappointment. When he died last year he was owner and publisher of the Arizona Daily Star, with a brilliant reputation as a newspaperman. I considered him to be the best-informed man in the country on foreign affairs and to draw the soundest conclusions from his information. Although domestically a Liberal, he was a good American in the international field. For himself and for his country, his falling out with Colonel Wise was, perhaps, most fortunate if that was the determining factor in his following a newspaper, rather than a military, career.

Frank: What was the Meuse-Argonne like? Was this a mass offensive?

Blake: Yes. It was very interesting. The attack was on a very narrow front. I think the regiment attacked on a two-battalion front and the battalions on a two-company front and the companies on a two-platoon front, so you can see how it narrowed. . . And then the artillery of the entire Army was behind that division. And when that bombardment opened, God and his thunder and lightning never did anything to equal it.

Frank: You never heard anything like it.

Blake: And behind the German lines these huge craters were lip to lip. It was a terrific thing, the most awesome thing I ever experienced. So there was comparatively little resistance. The Germans had wire, and the wire didn't seem to be damaged by the bombardment. The shells apparently landed just behind the German front-line position. Where I walked up, there was a machine gun right in front. It was still rather dark so that I could see the muzzle sparks. It stopped shooting and I went on up, walked right into a hole through the wire. It looked like a trap, for normally they would have something there when they withdrew to drop into it. So I went through to be sure it was all right before bringing any part of the company through it. The 17th Company was off to our right. I had the 66th Company then. And it was just like a picture you'd see in the *London Illustrated Review.* The Germans were standing up heaving hand grenades and their machine guns were shooting. So I scooted back through the wire and brought up the machine gun section that was attached to my company and set it up just inside the wire and started shooting down the line of trenches inside this wire – rolled it up like that.

Frank: Rolled up the flank.

Blake: Yeah, and the 17th Company – I don't think they knew what happened. I never said anything. I never even mentioned that until now. Their company commander was killed. But that was as beautiful an example of the effect of flanking with automatic fire on a position as I ever saw.

Frank: Well, you got a Navy Cross for an operation during the Belleau Wood action. That was when the wheat field was being swept by machine gun fire.

Blake: Well, yes. I was lucky.

Frank: I don't know about that. You maintained liaison with the 49th Company and continually crossing and recrossing an open field swept by machine gun fire, and your company was on the extreme left flank of the division, and you maintained liaison with the French unit on the left flank. So the Germans being as well dug in as they were at Belleau Wood, it must have been pretty difficult.

Blake: Well, it wasn't an organized trench system. They were just foxholes.

Frank: The Armistice took place shortly after the Meuse-Argonne. As a matter of fact, that was probably the last major operation of the war, wasn't it?

Blake: Yes. Actually, the Meuse-Argonne was the last operation of the war, because we fought right up until after the Armistice. Frank Whitehead and I got to the farmhouse (Senegal Farm) where the battalion headquarters was to be set up just a few minutes before 11 o'clock, and we were sitting there looking at our watches, we'd gotten the word unofficially and informally that the war was going to be over at 11 o'clock. That was the rumor. While we were sitting there, Charlie Dunbeck . . . (interruption) I believe I was saying that Frank Whitehead and I were sitting there by the side of the road looking at our watches, and at just about 11 o'clock a machine gun began to sputter down on our left front someplace. We said, "That sounds a hell of a lot like an armistice, doesn't it?" He'd been wounded in the Champagne and had picked up the rumor of the pending armistice on his way back to the company. Then Charlie Dunbeck came up this old farm road through the woods and said he'd received a report that one of his companies was surrounded in the village down the road – I forget the name of the village. It was quite foggy. He wanted one of us to go down and see if we could help them, so I said I'd go. By that time between the wounded and sick and exhausted, I had about 25 men left in the company. So we started down the road in single file through the fog. And after we got down a ways, I could hear the Germans shouting and wheels moving around. The column stopped. The word came back to send up an interpreter. I thought maybe Captain Dunbeck wanted to send somebody down through the woods to see if he could hear anything, pick up any information. We waited and waited and waited and nothing happened. So I got impatient and walked up to the head of the column, and there at the gates of this village – an old village that had apparently once been walled – Captain Dunbeck was standing with a short of half smile on his face, and across the road were a half a dozen Germans, no helmets, no arms, no anything. I said, "What goes on here?" He said, "These damn fools say the war is over." I said, "What are we going to do?" "Well," he said, "they don't care what we do. We can take them prisoner, do anything we want. They're through."

So we went back up the hill. Major Hamilton, who then was the battalion commander, had just arrived; and as I walked up, a runner handed him a message. I think it was about 1:30 then, and that was the official information that the war was over. So we were informed that the war was over two and a half hours afterwards, and we got our first word from the Germans.

Frank: Tight censorship on unit identification had been maintained by Pershing, but it was busted wide open supposedly with Floyd Gibbons' last dispatch was allowed through talking about Belleau Wood and the Marines, 5th and 6th Regiments of Marines; and it appeared that nearly everything after that, no matter who did it in the AEF was attributed to the Marines – or at least it was felt that way by some of the Army people. What was the reaction? Did you hear from home after that with considerable interest in what you were doing?

Blake: All I remember in that regard is a letter from my father saying from the casualty list it looked as if the Army was letting George do it. So I suppose the casualty lists at home identified Marines. I don't know how else he could have said that. That's all I remember in that regard.

Frank: After you got the word about the Armistice what did you do?

Blake: We stayed there that night. I'll never forget it – although we had orders to maintain a strict alert just as though the war was still on. That was impossible to do. I think every individual in the battalion built himself his own private fire.

Frank: For the first time in a long time.

Blake: Yes, the slopes on either side of the Meuse were just ablaze with lights. It looked almost like a city. Very cheerful.

Frank: Fraternization?

Blake: No, we didn't go that far. And shortly thereafter we moved into a village that had been occupied by the Germans throughout the war. The country was desolate. The people were sodden. I remember some French children playing on the outskirts of town. They were shooting flare pistols, German flare pistols, and talking in German.

Frank: The Germans had been there so long.

Blake: Yes, they'd been there throughout the war. No indication of animation of any sort on the part of the population. The only expression of any sort of thanksgiving at our coming and the war being over was from the mayor when the adjutant went to settle the bill for billets. He said, "We've kept the Germans here for four years for nothing. I guess we can keep you for a couple of nights for nothing." And then we started on to Germany and the bridgehead boundary. And crossing the line into Belgium was like passing from a land of desolation into a land of milk and honey.

Frank: Belgium hadn't been touched too heavily?

Blake: That part of Belgium, no. Crops were abundant; the people decorated the towns as we came through; met us at the edge of town singing and dancing. The war apparently had been very easy for them compared to France across the border.

Frank: What were the morale and the spirit of your Marines like? Now that the war was over, they wanted to get home or were they looking forward to the operation or what?

Blake: Well, they wanted to get home, but they were a well-disciplined organization. It didn't affect them any. I think they would have been glad to have marched right down to the pier and gone aboard and gone home, but they carried on just as though the war was still on from the point of view of discipline. No trouble.

Frank: You marched to where?

Blake: We crossed the Rhine at Remagen at the railroad bridge, which figured in the crossing in the last war. We spent the night in quite a nice little town on the right bank and then the next day went over the hill to the Wied Valley. The battalion headquarters was at Niederbreitbach, and I ended up in a very little village of 14 houses and 20 barns with 293 men and 14 officers on top of a windswept, cold hill; and we stayed there until we came home in July.

A very interesting occurrence during the advance in Meuse-Argonne was when we had been passed through and were in, I guess it was, the regimental reserve position resting under the reverse slope of a steep hill. I think perhaps I saw the last horse-drawn artillery in the American Army to displace forward at a full gallop under fire. It was very dramatic to see those – what must have been – eight horse teams with shrapnel. (It was real shrapnel, not fragmenting high explosive) bursting overhead. It looked like a Civil War painting.

Frank: Just the other night there was something on television repeating that British Broadcasting Company's television series on World War I. It was quite good. I don't know whether you've ever seen any part of that.

Blake: I think I saw it one night.

Frank: This was the battle of Verdun, and it showed the same thing – an excellent movie of the period showing the French horse-drawn artillery. Very dramatic, of course.

25

Side 2, Tape 1

Frank:	You went back, and of course those men who were to go home were mustered out at Quantico. Did you take part in the victory parade on Fifth Avenue in New York?
Blake:	Yes.
Frank:	That must have been quite stirring.
Blake:	Well, they'd had several parades already, and the New Yorkers were kind of tired of parades. There was a good turnout. Apparently we were a different breed of cats than they had been used to seeing. I remember it was a rather hot day.
Frank:	That was in August.
Blake:	And then men didn't fraternize in any way with the crowd as we went along, and every now and then I'd hear somebody say, "My, they look cross" or "they look stern." Then we paraded in Washington. That was a more enthusiastic crowd.
Frank:	That was at the time of the disbandment of the 4th Brigade, I think.
Blake:	Yes.
Frank:	President Wilson reviewed it together with General Lejeune.
Blake:	Yes, that's right. And when we pulled into the Washington railroad station – a train of 17th Field Artillery pulled by us slowly. I always remember them calling to us: "Goodbye, Marines." We got along very well with our artillery. They liked us because they said they felt the guns were safe. That's very important to an artilleryman.
Frank:	How did you look at them as far as giving you supporting fire?
Blake:	Wonderful.
Frank:	Of course, I don't think Marine artillery got into action in World War I.
Blake:	No.
Frank:	There was considerable controversy over this. There was a great deal of heartburn in the sense that it appeared the Army didn't trust Marine artillerymen.
Blake:	Well, there was hardly a place for it. The Army had to wrench their organization even to get the 4th Brigade in, because we didn't have the personnel we have now to form a division.
Frank:	Well, it was very fortunate for the Marine Corps that Marines were sent over.
Blake:	Oh, yes. General Barnett deserves a tremendous amount of credit for that. I don't think there's any doubt that on account of that effort of his, he is responsible for making the Marine Corps develop as it has.

<u>Peacetime Marine Captain 1919-1932</u>

Frank:	Were you aware of the controversy surrounding the release for Barnett as commandant?
Blake:	Oh, yes, very much so.
Frank:	How so?
Blake:	Well, I was at Quantico in close contact with General Butler, and General Butler was a 100% extrovert; and anything that General Butler believed, everybody knew about.
Frank:	There was no secret about his attempts to get rid of Barnett?
Blake:	No.
Frank:	It was done on the up and up, insofar as an operation like that could be on the up and up.
Blake:	Yes.
Frank:	Do you thing Lejeune was privy to it?
Blake:	Well, I don't know. I don't know what he could have done about it if he were.
Frank:	He could have said, "I want no part of it," even though it meant that he would not become the next commandant.
Blake:	Well, that's hard to say. Congressman Butler was a very, very powerful man. I would hesitate to put any sort of a finger on General Lejeune. He was a most admirable character.
Frank:	The Marine Corps in the '20s and following that in the image that he wanted it to be fashioned in, he certainly took hold – it would appear.
Blake:	Of course, General Butler, with all his political influence and perhaps discreditable attributes, was a very dramatic figure. He may well have saved the Marine Corps then when it looked as though it was going to be scuttled.
Frank:	Was Butler well liked?
Blake:	Yes and no. I liked him very much. An interesting character.
Frank:	Would you say he was the Puller of his day in a sense, that he was either liked or disliked with no in between? That's if you can attribute this to Puller also.
Blake:	Well, that's hard to say. I never knew of any Marine who disliked General Puller, and I knew plenty who disliked General Butler heartily. But the two of them had much in common in that they were both dramatic, aggressive and outspoken figures.
Frank:	I didn't mean to put you on the spot by getting your attitudes on General Puller, but he was controversial; and I think there's very much a similarity between the two of them in that sense. Well, what did you

	do after you got back to Quantico? I see you went home for about three months.
Blake:	I was out here on duty at Mare Island. Then the girl to whom I'd become engaged to be married had gone to Washington to work during the war as her part of the war effort. She was still there. So I got leave and went back to see her at Christmastime, went down to Headquarters Marine Corps and they were opening an officers' school at Quantico. I got assigned to it and went to school there.
Frank:	Had you become a regular by this time?
Blake:	Oh, yes. Yes, I was sworn into the regular Marine Corps – I think it was September 1917. We went in as reserves just so we could go into training right away.
Frank:	So you determined that that was the career you wanted to make. What was your major at the University?
Blake:	I had planned to take up law.
Frank:	Had you done any law work at all?
Blake:	Just pre legal.
Frank:	Of course Leo Hermle had his doctorate already.
Blake:	No. He had taken one year of law. I should have, but I didn't. Then I went to the guard company, which I guess is the M.P. Company.
Frank:	At Quantico.
Blake:	Yes, and just the usual routine.
Frank:	This was the first officers' school after the war, though.
Blake:	Yes, it was the beginning of the present Marine Corps Schools.
Frank:	Oh, really? Who had it at that time, do you recall?
Blake:	Major Dyer? I'm not sure.
Frank:	It wasn't Dion Williams?
Blake:	Oh, no.
Frank:	He was a B.G. by then, wasn't he?
Blake:	Yes, I think so. No, it wasn't Dion Williams. I just don't remember.
Frank:	Was the course long?
Blake:	As I remember, it was much the same as the course I had gone through in the summer of 1917. They changed it a little. It was a little better.
Frank:	By this time the Russell Board had met, I think. The first board was the Russell Board?
Blake:	Yes. It was in the process of meeting. I forget whether that met in 1920. Around 1920, I think.
Frank:	Well, there were two boards that met.
Blake:	That's right. You're right. The Russell Board met immediately after the war.

Frank:	I forget the name of who had the second board. (Neville) Evidently the Russell Board did not satisfy the World War I veterans.
Blake:	Well, it didn't satisfy Smedley Butler.
Frank:	That was the reason. And then the Neville Board met. Neville must have had the second board.
Blake:	I don't know whether he actually sat on that board or not. I forget, quite frankly.
Frank:	Well, you were commissioned a captain in May of '21 with rank from June 1920. Did it come as a result of the Russell Board or the second board?
Blake:	You see, just on seniority I held my rank under the Russell Board. I think all the Russell Board did was eliminate certain officers.
Frank:	But then many of them came back with the second board and retained their lineal precedence even though they'd been out for a while.
Blake:	Or went up higher.
Frank:	You were number nine in the list of captains.
Blake:	Nine or ten. That was on the second board, I think.
Frank:	That didn't mean that you were going to make major any sooner.
Blake:	I made a few numbers on it.
Frank:	When did you make major actually? Was it before the selection board system went into effect?
Blake:	I don't remember.
Frank:	Yes, it must have been 1932. I have it right before me here, sir.
Blake:	I remember that somebody retired unexpectedly and I didn't get my pay cut. Or rather I got paid with my promotion. Hoover as an economy measure did away with all pay on promotion, and I just made it.
Frank:	He forced a 15% cut, I think it was.
Blake:	That also, yes.
Frank:	In 1922 you were assigned a very interesting duty in May. You were assigned to the *Henderson* as aide-de-camp to the Secretary of the Navy on a cruise to Japan.
Blake:	No, I had the Marine detachment on the *Henderson*, and he took me up to Peking with him. That was a temporary assignment, but my job was as Marine detachment commander on the *Henderson* that was put on the *Henderson* for that trip. The class of '81 was holding its reunion in Japan as the guest of a Japanese admiral who had been in the class at the Naval Academy, so he invited his classmates to hold their reunion there.
Frank:	And the *Henderson* was made available to transport them.
Blake:	Yes. And the Secretary took the opportunity to revisit China, so the trip was made a little more extensive than it would have been otherwise.

Frank:	But actually this was only about a six-month assignment.
Blake:	Yes, even less.
Frank:	Highly ceremonial, I suppose.
Blake:	Well, as a matter of fact, everything was rather informal. I don't know. It was very interesting.
Frank:	Anything unusual happen during this period that sticks in your mind about the particular tour?
Blake:	No, I don't think so. It was all very strange and very interesting to me. On the trip from Peking to Shanghai, I understand that due to the civil war that was constantly going on in China, that was the last train that made the trip for a long, long time.
Frank:	You went seagoing on your next assignment then.
Blake:	Yes, I had the detachment in the *Pennsylvania*.
Frank:	You served in the *Pennsylvania*. Anything unusual about this seagoing tour?
Blake:	No, I don't think so.
Frank:	Strictly a west coast . . .
Blake:	Except for the cruise to the Caribbean. I think we made two Caribbean cruises.
Frank:	Were you berthed in Long Beach?
Blake:	Yes. At San Pedro.
Frank:	Of course, this was the heyday of the battleship. Was the *Pennsylvania* a relatively new ship?
Blake:	No, the *Pennsylvania* was a sister ship of the *Arizona*. It was a standby fleet flagship; it had huge flag quarters. It was a very comfortable ship.
Frank:	Who was the fleet Marine officer at this time, do you remember?
Blake:	No, I don't. I haven't the slightest idea. General Shepherd might remember. He and General Cates were also in the fleet at the time.
Frank:	You commanded the detachment.
Blake:	Commanded a detachment on the *Pennsylvania*.
Frank:	Who were the officers you had under you, do you recall?
Blake:	Roberts, who was killed on Okinawa, was my j.o.
Frank:	Did he have his big moustache at this time?
Blake:	He had a little moustache. I think John Bushrod Wilson was there. He had a heart attack while hunting a few years ago at Camp Pendleton. He was my first j.o.
Frank:	This was rather select duty, was it not, at this time?
Blake:	Well, I imagine it was.
Frank:	It was a necessary duty for the career pattern, though.

Blake:	It was very advisable, yes. I'm sure they tried to assign officers whom they thought would make a creditable showing in the Navy.
Frank:	Was there some controversy that the Navy had a power of veto over Marine officers who were assigned to sea duty at this time?
Blake:	To my knowledge, no. Of course, if they didn't like the one who was sent after he got there, I suppose there would have been no problem about having him relieved; but that applies practically any place.
Frank:	Sea duty was a desirable duty, was it not?
Blake:	Yes indeed.
Frank:	You had only this one tour, I believe. Or did you have another one?
Blake:	I was Squadron Marine Officer to the special service squadron.
Frank:	In the Caribbean later on.
Blake:	Yes. From about '35 to about '37.
Frank:	We're a little ahead of ourselves. You remained in the *Pennsylvania* for about two years, and then went to Mare Island again. You did a considerable amount of duty on the west coast, did you not?
Blake:	No, very little, as a matter of fact. I did this one tour of duty. I was there at Mare Island for a few months, and then I went to Goat Island to command the detachment at the receiving station and duty as judge advocate. That was my only tour of west coast duty apart from sea service.
Frank:	You remained there for nearly three years. You joined the Marine detachment at the receiving station in November of '25 and you left in January of '28. A considerable amount of court martial activities, was there not?
Blake:	I was judge advocate of the general court.
Frank:	And that kept you busy?
Blake:	Oh, yes. That was my main job there.
Frank:	What was the general nature of the offenses?
Blake:	I imagine desertion was the majority of the cases. There was one case of a petty officer in the supply corps who was charged with accepting money from enlisted men for doing them favors. Cases of that sort were very rare. By and large they were routine desertion cases.
Frank:	Had the Butler case down at San Diego occurred at this time when you were there?
Blake:	Oh, I forgot about that. I don't remember. As a matter of fact, I forget what the Butler case was. That was charging Colonel Williams with being drunk?
Frank:	Yes.
Blake:	That had completely and totally slipped my mind.

Frank: I understood that it became quite a cause celebre I guess all over the country as well as on the west coast.

Blake: It did. I imagine it was because Colonel Williams was a popular officer, and a lot of people didn't like General Butler.

Frank: I imagine there was considerable side taking.

Blake: On that account, yes. I always had the impression that General Butler acted very unwillingly and that his hand was pretty much forced. But people didn't like him and didn't want to see it that way.

Frank: In January you were assigned to the 2nd Brigade, which was then in Nicaragua. You were assigned to the 11th Regiment. Was that an artillery regiment at that time?

Blake: No.

Frank: Infantry. And you became the battalion exec. Was that at Chinandega?

Blake: No, we first went to Leon and from Leon we took a large bull cart convoy up to Ocotal. As I remember, the battalion didn't go into Ocotal. We stopped at Pueblo Nuevo and diverted to Condega. Whether we sent the bull carts on with a guard or not, I don't remember. At Pueblo Nuevo, which is about 30 miles south of Ocotal, we were sent over to a God-forsaken little hole of Condega. Battalion headquarters stayed there for a little while and then went down to Esteli which is about 35 miles toward Managua by trail.

Frank: Who was the commander of the battalion at this time?

Blake: Major Pierce, Biff Pierce. I forget what his initials were.

Frank: I've heard him referred to as Biff Pierce.

Blake: A very nice gentleman.

Frank: And the regimental commander was who?

Blake: The regimental commander was Colonel Dunlap. The brigade commander was General Feland.

Frank: Logan Feland. Who were some of your company officers in the battalion?

Blake: Bill McNulty, now dead.

Frank: This was the father of World War II, or was he the one who was captured on Guam?

Blake: He was the one who was captured on Guam.

Frank: His father was a colonel, I believe, in the Marine Corps.

Blake: His father-in-law was Alice Lee's father. I wish I had a better memory for names than I have. George McHenry, a very fine active officer. He's dead, I think. J.D. Smith; he became a brigadier during the war. He's dead. John O'Neill was our battalion surgeon. It was he who made the

	patrol with Captain O'Shea who got in quite a fight. General Atkinson. He's retired now down in San Diego. I wish I could remember more.
Frank:	Was that Louis Atkinson?
Blake:	They called him "Benny" Atkinson. I forget his initials.
Frank:	What was the situation in Nicaragua at this time?
Blake:	Well, there were small groups of bandits around. Sandino was operating in the hills along the Honduran border. They were generally unsettled because of that. But when Somoza eliminated Sandino, why Nicaragua quieted down.
Frank:	Did you work closely with the Guardia?
Blake:	I don't remember. I don't remember that there was any Guardia Nacional any places that we were. I think by and large any cooperation with the Guardia would be on a higher level. But so far as the operating units were concerned, I don't think so.
Frank:	What was the duty like in these days?
Blake:	Well, no place in which you operate in the field is particularly pleasant. So far as bugs are concerned, North Carolina is a lot worse. Bugs and snakes are worse in the Middle Atlantic States than any place I've ever been. There were very few mosquitoes. The difference is that the mosquitoes in Nicaragua in the hills were not pests as mosquitoes, but the few that there were carried malaria; and the same goes for the South Pacific.
Frank:	I see a very interesting note here. On March 18th, 1929, you were placed under arrest for a period of five days for undiplomatic and rude conduct toward an officer of the Nicaraguan volunteer forces at Samoto, Nicaragua. What were the circumstances of that incident?
Blake:	Well, I'd rather skip that.
Frank:	Was that a Marine officer or a Nicaraguan?
Blake:	No, a Nicaraguan.
Frank:	The language, "undiplomatic and rude conduct" I felt was probably diplomatically put.
Blake:	It was.
Frank:	All right, sir. Well, that didn't seem to have any disability as far as your career was concerned, because you took over the battalion in April of 1929 and then went back to the States in August. Anything unusual that comes to your mind about this tour in Nicaragua? Was it just a regular tour with the brigade?
Blake:	I would say so.
Frank:	There wasn't too much action at this period.
Blake:	No.

Frank:	Somoza had pretty well strengthened the government and Sandino was on the run.
Blake:	Moncada was still president then. Somoza followed Moncada, but I forget just when he went in.
Frank:	Well, had you made many patrols with the battalion?
Blake:	A number.
Frank:	There was no punitive action, no combat fighting, at this time?
Blake:	Very little.
Frank:	The aviation was pretty active down in Nicaragua at the time.
Blake:	Oh, aviation was a lifesaver. It would have been extremely difficult just from a logistic point of view without aviation.
Frank:	Did you ever get the bug to learn how to fly?
Blake:	No.
Frank:	Did you become a polo player, an equestrian at this time?
Blake:	No.
Frank:	You went back to Quantico in September to attend a field officers' course, did you not?
Blake:	I think so.
Frank:	Do you remember the curriculum at all?
Blake:	Well, it was precisely the same at that time as the command and staff school and Fort Leavenworth.
Frank:	The instructors were graduates of the Fort Leavenworth Course?
Blake:	Whether they all were or not, I don't know, but a number of them were.
Frank:	Your schooling was interrupted to take part in the electoral commission down there at Nicaragua, was it not?
Blake:	Yes, I served at the electoral mission in 1930 and 1932. I was chairman of the departmental board of elections, the department of Masaya in 1930, and I was secretary of the national board of elections in '32.
Frank:	Had you learned Spanish when you were down there?
Blake:	I worked at it. I got so I could get along a little bit, got very much interested in it.
Frank:	Going back to the field officers' course, do you remember who some of your instructors were?
Blake:	General Hermle, Charlie Barrett. I can remember their faces, and I can't remember their names.
Frank:	About this time I think General Russell was commandant, was he not, in 1930?
Blake:	He may have been.

Frank: This period was more or less a turning point so far as the Marine Corps was concerned, was it not, regarding the development of amphibious warfare doctrine?

Blake: Yes. They were just working on it there. I wish I could remember the name of the officer who was working that up. His name slips my mind.

Frank: Was del Valle down there at the time working on it?

Blake: At this time, no.

Frank: Worton?

Blake: No.

Frank: Ellis Bell Miller?

Blake: E.B. Miller. He, he came later. The other Miller was one of the instructors there in the command and staff school era of the Marine Corps school. E.B. Miller came when they'd started developing amphibious warfare. At that time the schools were in the old double deckers down behind post headquarters, and it was when the schools had moved into the new brick buildings that they really started seriously on amphibious warfare.

Frank: Was Peck there at this time?

Blake: He may have been – I don't remember. I remember him over at the other schools after we got into amphibious warfare.

Frank: Do you remember a Naval officer by the name of Walter Ansel?

Blake: I remember the name. I can't see his face. And when he was there, I don't remember.

Frank: In the instruction you had, was there much about the advanced base concept?

Blake: At that time, no.

Frank: In other words, the field officers' course, mainly staff functioning and so on, preparing you for the next higher echelon.

Blake: Well, it was studying combat of the field officer on a higher level.

Frank: Off and on you had the school and then the electoral commission. Then in 1931 you went to the Spanish language course. But let's talk a little bit about supervising the elections, because I think this was an interesting era for the Marine Corps.

Blake: It was very interesting.

Frank: What was the nature of your duties?

Blake: On the departmental board of elections it was largely seeing that the elections were conducted fairly and that no undue pressure was brought to bear on the electorate by the administration. The conservatives were out; it was primarily from the conservatives that complaints came. And of course they take their elections very seriously; the priests down

35

	there were largely conservatives. It so happened that I was away, but the priest at Masaya invited me to a party that he was giving. I would have gone if I had been there. The liberals reported me to the head of the electoral commission for favoring the conservatives by going to this party. It was that kind of stuff that you were always up against.
Frank:	Was there any gunfire?
Blake:	I don't remember anything of that nature. The principal problem was presented by investigating complaints registered by the conservative political leaders of the community, most of which were fabricated.
Frank:	Would you say this was probably the most honest election that Nicaragua had?
Blake:	Oh, I'm sure they were – the ones that were supervised by us. I don't know what has gone on since, but I wouldn't doubt that they were. Even the Mexicans said that they were honest.
Frank:	I suppose that's a commentary of some sort.
Blake:	Well, they were looking for trouble.
Frank:	The Mexicans were?
Blake:	Oh, sure.
Frank:	Were they part of the electoral commission also?
Blake:	No.
Frank:	But the Mexicans had supported Sandino, had they not?
Blake:	Yes.
Frank:	I think the Mexican government at this time was quite liberal, quite radical.
Blake:	Yes, but they probably would have anyway. We don't get along too well with the Latin Americans. We think differently.
Frank:	Were you the first officer to be assigned to the Spanish language course, or had you had some predecessors?
Blake:	The group that I went over with was the first.
Frank:	Who else went over with you?
Blake:	Maurice Holmes, Blythe Jones, Don Kendall.
Frank:	Just the four of you – and your families.
Blake:	Yes.
Frank:	You went to Madrid.
Blake:	We all went to Madrid, and then after the summer session was over at the University, I went up to Salamanca. The rest of them stayed in Madrid.
Frank:	And you studied up in Salamanca?
Blake:	Yes.
Frank:	Were you assigned there?

Blake: No, you could go any place you wanted to. We were given no instructions whatsoever.

Frank: Was it formal instruction up at Salamanca?

Blake: Yes. All the universities had a course for foreigners, and I registered at the University in their course for foreigners, which gave me admission as an auditor to any courses I wanted to audit and also gave me a private tutor for a very small amount, because I was the only student in the class – and he was a very interesting little chap. And then in addition to that, I took lessons on the side.

Frank: How competent did you become in the language?

Blake: Moderately so. I could read without much difficulty, and when I'm in practice speak a fairly fluent broken Spanish.

Frank: Have you used it since that time?

Blake: Oh, yes. I still read.

Frank: You still read in Spanish and keep up your proficiency.

Blake: Write to friends over there.

Frank: In Spain. The Marine Corps was considerably interested in language training for officers at this time, was it not?

Blake: Yes. Everybody had to take a correspondence course in Spanish. If anybody got anything out of it, I don't know. They also taught it at the Marine Corps Schools. Of course, at this time our activity in Latin America was drawing to a close. It's unfortunate they didn't start it a hundred years ago.

Frank: But a number of people went to study French.

Blake: That was in connection with their attendance at the Ecole de Guerre.

Frank: How about Chinese?

Blake: Yes. They had quite a few Chinese, and I believe they had some Japanese students.

Frank: And Russian?

Blake: I don't know about Russian. Arthur Worton I think studied Chinese.

Frank: Yes. I think General Holcomb was the first Chinese language student.

Blake: That's right.

Field Officer 1932-1941

Frank: Did the Marine Corps ever make use of your Spanish language facility
            after that?

Blake: The Marine Corps itself, no. I taught it at the Marine Corps Schools.
            I went on my second tour with the electoral commission after that. I
            was assigned to Admiral Kimmel's staff when he made his trip around
            South America with a division of heavy cruisers. When was that? In
            '30 . . .

Frank: In '35?

Blake: No.

Frank: '36 was the goodwill cruise.

Blake: No. In '36 I was in the special service squadron. It must have been '39
            or '40.

Frank: March '39. You went to Cuba.

Blake: I joined the ship at Guantanamo Bay.

Frank: You went from New York to Cuba on the S.S. *Del Oriente.* You were
            over in Spain for a year or more.

Blake: Thirteen months, I believe.

Frank: And then went back to the electoral mission. And during '32, of course,
            you received your majority.

Blake: Yes, I was sworn in in Managua.

Frank: That must have been a nice gift.

Blake: It was.

Frank: Unanticipated?

Blake: No.

Frank: You knew where your number was. Once the selection board system
            came in, you just received your lineal precedence, and then when you
            were due for consideration for lieutenant colonel, you'd just come up
            under that system.

Blake: Yes.

Frank: After you completed your electoral commission duties, you went
            to Quantico. You joined the Marine Corps Schools' detachment in
            December of '32 for duty on a special board. What was that special
            board, do you recall?

Blake: Frankly, no.

Frank: It was only two months. Then you became an instructor in the field
            officers' course. What did you teach?

Blake: Communications, tactical communications – nothing technical.

Frank: What prepared you for this particular course?

Blake: Nothing. I had to go and dig out of a book what I had already learned at Marine Corps schools.

Frank: Did you take over the course, notes and so on of the previous instructor?

Blake: I presume I did. I don't remember.

Frank: Do you remember who some of the other instructors were in the field officers' course at this time?

Blake: Lyle Miller.

Frank: I was trying to think of his name. He was one of those who was involved in the development of amphibious warfare. There was a board, I think, of del Valle, Lyle Miller, Peck and Walter Ansel. It may have been just about this time, maybe a little earlier.

Blake: Charlie Barrett.

Frank: That's right, Charlie Barrett.

Blake: DeWitt Peck, Pete del Valle. E.B. Miller was executive officer. General Breckinridge was commandant of the schools.

Frank: I think Walter Ansel was a Navy number on the . . .

Blake: He may have been there at that time. I remember there was a very good and interested Naval officer on the staff at that time. I don't remember what his name was.

Frank: He was about the only one. It was almost a kiss of death for any of the Navy types who were involved.

Blake: Yes.

Frank: During this time in November or September of '33, the Fleet Marine Force was formed; and General Navy Order Number 5 I believe was enacted in November of '33 or signed by the Secretary of the Navy, which in essence approved this. Which then meant that considerable doctrinal writings had to be done. They had to start developing this concept. Were you involved with it at all? Do you remember this period?

Blake: I frankly don't. I know there was a lot of work in connection with it that went on at the schools, and they began to orient their teaching around amphibious tactics and small wars. There was a great deal of discussion on the type of craft that would be used.

Frank: Were you used to write the landing party manual at all? Did you get involved with that?

Blake: That I don't remember.

Frank: In other words, the forerunner of what appeared in FTP 167, I believe, was developed at this time. What I'm trying to clarify, especially with those people who were involved at Quantico at that time . . . I've read some place and someone has written the fact that the school

39

	shut down, and everybody was put to work doing this. I can't seem to clarify this.
Blake:	I don't remember that.
Frank:	It must have been earlier. It had to be.
Blake:	Of course, General Barrett to me was the spark of genius in that work. I felt that he didn't get the credit that he should have. I may not have the right slant on it. Perhaps I don't know enough about it. But to me he was the spark of genius.
Frank:	I think this is very largely true, because anyone else who was involved has attributed to him being the driving force in this particular area, and also being a great driving force as far as the development of Naval gunfire support is concerned.
Blake:	Yes. And his concept of landing operations has not essentially changed to this day, and it was right there at the Marine Corps Schools that the Normandy beaches were made possible.
Frank:	Did you know Earl Ellis at all?
Blake:	Oh, yes. He was the executive officer of the 5th Marines during the occupation of Germany. He was a wonderful person.
Frank:	What kind of an individual was he, a brilliant individual?
Blake:	Oh, yes. And he had a wonderful personality. He exuded confidence. I just didn't understand what happened to him, didn't understand him taking that turn.
Frank:	There was nothing in the earlier days to indicate that . . .
Blake:	From what I saw of him. I never saw him under the influence of liquor. As a matter of fact, I don't remember seeing him ever take a drink, but that doesn't mean anything.
Frank:	He was very close to General Lejeune, I understand.
Blake:	I'm sure he was – and General Feland.
Frank:	His death in the '20s then out in the Pacific came as quite a surprise to everybody? Or did you even know about it?
Blake:	Johnny Selden told me about some intelligence work that he was engaged on in the Pacific. I'm very vague. But having heard what he was doing and some concept of the risks involved, I wouldn't say it was a surprise – no.

Tape 2, Side 1

Blake:	I think it's the loyalty of men to their comrades and to their company that is of extreme importance to development of military spirit. In World War I, the Marine brigade was extremely fortunate in that all its men, after they had been sent to the hospital, came back to the brigade and were reassigned to their old companies. That's where their friends

were. Their company was their home. They would run away from the hospitals; they would run away from duty assignments in rear areas to come back to their companies – not because they wanted to get into combat and go out and get killed but because they were homesick for their companies and where their friends were. And it made for a tremendous spirit and a tremendous sense of unit that is lacking when men are sent back to duty in different regiments each time they come out of the hospital. Of course, once in a while you would run across queer characters that just seemed to like battle. I knew of three in the 17th Company. One was a youngster from apparently a nice family in the middle economic brackets. One was a French Canadian lumberjack from Minnesota. And one was just a bum from off the streets from God knows where. They were a trio who ran around together. They would go AWOL after every battle and then come back in time for the next one. They missed most of Soissons, and they told me it was because they were in the brig in Bordeaux when they heard about it, and they had trouble getting out of that brig and getting back. How in the world they heard about it down in Bordeaux, when even we who were in the regiment didn't know that the attack was going to take place until we got there, is beyond me. But that's all part of the spirit that goes to make up a successful organization.

We had one little Jewish newsboy from Philadelphia in the 66th Company who was an automatic rifleman. His name was Abie Strauss, and he was known amongst the men as Abie Strauss, the Goiman killer. He wasn't much bigger than a Chauchat gun. He was evacuated during the Meuse-Argonne. At the beginning of the occupation of Germany, you practically had to have a set of orders signed by General Pershing himself before you could get into the occupied zone. And one day from my hilltop at Wolfenacker, I saw this little figure coming up the hill from Niederbreitbach, and it was Abie. He was homesick for the company and wanted to get back where his friends were, and he ran away from the hospital that he was in. When I saw him I said, "Where's all your equipment, Abie?" He said, "I've got me toothbrush, Cap'n." I said, "How in the world did you get here?" "Well," he said, "I just got on a train. The M.P.s would get on at one end and I at the rear end and start walking through, I'd just walk on forward. Before they got to me, I'd manage to get off and get on the rear end again. I got here." Those are some of the things that I think are so important in making the spirit of the regiment. As I said, forward of the 75s, there's no such thing as patriotism. It's guts, discipline, comradeship, and loyalty to your comrades that keeps the men going and sends them forward.

Frank: Those three men who you were talking about sound very much like Kipling's "Soldiers Three." Did you know John Thomason at this point?

Blake: Oh, yes, very well.

Frank: Did you ever get any prints from him? Did he ever give you any of the things he did that never before had been published?

Blake: I remember he did an illustration of Frankie and Johnny and the Bastard King of England. The Bastard King of England was a terrific thing. I don't know whether he did.

Frank: Well, we've been talking about these people. Thomason you said you knew quite well. Of course, he became a quite popular and well-accepted writer. Let's get back to the field officers' course. You were teaching Spanish; you were also teaching tactical communications. What else were you doing at this period?

Blake: Frankly, I don't remember.

Frank: It was kind of a quiet period, was it not, in the sense that it was the lull before the storm in a way?

Blake: Oh, yes.

Frank: It seems to me from what I've heard that the choice duty at this period of time was China.

Blake: Well, of course, the Peking garrison was always considered choice duty – at the legation. I don't know about Shanghai, whether that was particularly choice from the point of view of living or not.

(A third person in the room speaks at some length but it is not articulate) (Elynor Blake)

      She's speaking of people who have lived all their lives in China in relative luxury – how upsetting it has been for them to have to leave China and those conditions.

Frank: Of course, this happened with the group that had to leave both before World War II and then who finally left in 1949.

      Now, in June 1934, you were the chief of the F-1 and F-2 sections at the schools. At least that's what you're down here as.

Blake: It's probably true. I don't remember what we did.

Frank: You went on temporary duty with Naval Intelligence in Washington at this time. Do you recall for what reason?

Blake: I had the Latin American desk in ONI from the time I was detached from the Special Service Squadron until I went to the Naval War College in the fall of 1940.

Frank: Well, this was in June of '35. Was this perhaps in anticipation of assignment as the Squadron Marine Officer in the *Trenton?*

Blake: How long was I on that?

Frank:	Just from 3 to 14 June of 1935, about two weeks, less than two weeks.
Blake:	In 1935?
Frank:	Yes, sir.
Blake:	It's possible that we were going up to the Naval War College to give a presentation and that I remember. I was doing intelligence work at the Marine Corps schools, and I know that I went up ONI to see what I could find out about Truk. Now, whether that was the occasion or not, I don't know.
Frank:	Well, you were working on those problems at this time – Truk, Guam, the Palaus and so on. There were advance base problems and so on. This was the period when that developed. Who relieved you as chief of F-2, General Erskine?
Blake:	I think he did. He must have, because he was with me when I had that section.
Frank:	Who had the F-3 section, do you recall?
Blake:	It might have been DeWitt Peck. It might have been Houston Noble. I don't think it was Lyle Miller. Or it could have been General Smith, Julian Smith.
Frank:	Well, in any case you left there in July, and you went down through the Canal Zone to join the *Trenton,* and then you made lieutenant colonel. You were Squadron Marine Officer. What were the nature of your duties primarily? What were your duties?
Blake:	Look out for the interests of the Marine detachment.
Frank:	That was it primarily?
Blake:	I've never see the duties of a Squadron Division Marine Officer outlined. But that is practically what his job is and go around with the admiral when he wants you to, play golf with the admiral if he is a golfer.
Frank:	How many ships were in the squadron at the time, do you recall?
Blake:	Three: two destroyers and the flagship, which was a light cruiser.
Frank:	So you only had one ship's detachment actually.
Blake:	They had Marines on each destroyer. One of the ship's divisions was the Marines.
Frank:	Wasn't that unusual?
Blake:	Very unusual.
Frank:	Why did they have detachments on the destroyers?
Blake:	Because they wanted that many Marines in case it was necessary to make a landing.
Frank:	Was the squadron the only fleet unit in the area?
Blake:	Yes, permanently.

Frank:	This was the permanent special squadron.
Blake:	Yes.
Frank:	Whom did you relieve as Squadron Marine Officer?
Blake:	Creasey.
Frank:	And who relieved you?
Blake:	Don Kendall.
Frank:	Was there anything unique in this two-year tour?
Blake:	Nothing. It was just the customary champagne cruise, the things you do on a job of that nature – drinking warm champagne on the beach at nine o'clock in the morning.
Frank:	Well, the sun was over the yardarm someplace in the world.
Blake:	Well, you wouldn't be aboard ship, of course, but you'd go ashore to make calls.
Frank:	You then began about a three-year tour of duty in Washington working out of Washington, in Washington with ONI.
Blake:	Yes, I had the Latin American desk, as it was called then.
Frank:	As a lieutenant colonel.
Blake:	Yes.
Frank:	What were your primary concerns at this time?
Blake:	Well, the handling of the Naval missions in Latin America came under that desk then. The Naval attaches came under that desk. Both our attaches in Latin America, and liaison with the Latin American Naval attaches in Washington. Anything they wanted from the Navy Department, they'd come and see me. It was very interesting work. We had authorized . . . As a matter of fact, when I went there the Brazilians were already building three destroyers of the Mahan type with our aid. Many problems came up in connection with that. The principal one was obtaining the 5-inch .38 all-purpose guns for them.
Frank:	Was that pretty restricted as far as the United States Navy was concerned?
Blake:	Yes. And worse than that, it was only made in the Naval gun factory. In fact, there were no private ordnance plants operating in the United States. The Nye Committee had just about put the quietus on the munitions industry in the United States, and it later became even more embarrassing. Our problem was how to carry out our promise to the Brazilian government to provide the 5-inch .38s for those ships without an act of Congress that might have been very difficult to obtain. I don't know how they finally solved it. I think that what everyone would have like to have seen done, from the President down, was to have had the chief of the bureau of ordnance stick his neck out and go ahead and sell them guns manufactured by the Naval gun factory. But the chief

of the bureau at that time was a very capable, very strong-minded, obstinate Dutchman, and he said, "If somebody will give me the order to provide them, I'll be happy to give them; but the appropriation act of Congress forbids the Naval appropriations being used for any other than U.S. purposes, so I can't do it." It went all the way up to President Roosevelt, who is reputed to have stated something to the effect about them trying to put him in jail. But I think they finally got a chief of the bureau that in view of the fact that the consensus was that they should have it, that nobody was going to lower the boom on anybody for doing it, and they got their guns.

Frank: Any Congressional reaction to it?

Blake: None whatsoever. It was very interesting, because at the time I got there, all the higher echelons in the Navy Department that had anything to do with the decision to give them those plans to build the ships with had been changed. They had to be briefed from the bottom up. When you try to get something cleared around through the various bureaus – everybody was brand new – it isn't easy. I had first of all to educate myself, and if you've ever tried to get anything out of the Navy Department files, you'll know what the problem was. The statement has been made that a message center is a place where everything is initially lost for three days. That's nothing compared to the Navy Department files. I found that the only way I could get correspondence even out of the ONI files – and the Navy Department files are vastly worse – was to have the date and the file number of the letter that I wanted. Then I could get it. I gradually educated myself on the *Mahan* destroyers and got the files straightened out so that we could look it up. That was an extremely interesting time. That was the type of stuff that we did.

Frank: At this time, of course, the threat from Europe was becoming increased, and also there was some indication of infiltration of the Axis powers in Latin America itself. Did this matter come under your cognizance also?

Blake: Yes.

Frank: In what way and what steps did you have to take?

Blake: Well, merely to try to get what information we could on it. Probably the best work was done by Don Kendall in the Canal Zone, who lined things up very beautifully. I forget all the details of it, but he got a lot of information on their activities there. Of course, there was an awful lot of stuff that was eyewash. The establishment of bases was constantly being reported. They finally sent a couple of Naval officers – I forget whether they were active or retired – who were yachtsmen on a cruise

45

down the Caribbean to see if they could find the submarine base that was supposed to be around Cozumel Island off the N.E. Coast of the Yucatan Peninsula somewhere. It was not so. There were submarines reported off the South American coast in the Pacific by commercial aviators, locations where a submarine couldn't get to from Germany; and I presume it was because they just confused the superstructure of a submarine with the deckhouse of a fishing vessel. That's the only thing I could see.

Frank: Or large whales.

Blake: Possibly. And then the *New York Times* had a big story in its magazine section on a German base in Peru, I think it was, in a place called Malabrigo – how they had it all fenced with barbed wire and German-uniformed sentries walking the post. Of course, in the first place, Malabrigo, which means "bad harbor," would not be any place for the Germans to want to establish a submarine base. That was hot air. But we were constantly bombarded with things of that nature.

Then the oil confiscation took place at that time.

Frank: Mexican.

Blake: Yes. And the representatives of the oil companies were always coming down to see the Chief of Naval Intelligence with stories on this, that and the other thing, frequently with uprisings that were about to take place in Mexico that never materialized. I remember getting a letter from the commander of the battleship division, who had been well documented on a lot of things that weren't going to happen in Mexico in the way of uprisings. Why he hadn't been informed. Well, at that time the nonintervention protocol of Buenos Aires had been in effect since 16 September 1937, and they were in the process of strengthening it in what later became the Charter of the Organization of American States. So Admiral Anderson sent it to me and said to prepare a reply. I just said, "There is not going to be revolution in Mexico, and if it did take place, the United States would not intervene because of the provisions of the nonintervention protocol of Buenos Aires, which we follow."

Admiral Anderson liked short letters. When he got that, he sent for me and said, "This is the best letter which has been put on my desk since I've been here."

Frank: Did the Marine aviation mission to Peru come under your cognizance?

Blake: It came under the cognizance of that desk. I'm just trying to think . . .

Frank: That's the one that "Nuts" Moore, General Moore . . .

Blake: I think that was negotiated while I was there. We tried to get one, and I think we got it, to Colombia. They were interested in Marines because they felt that our type of limited operations, as it were, was suited to their needs. They weren't interested in strategic bombing, which is the prime reason for the existence of a separate air force in this country.

Frank: Did you get reports in from FBI agents who had been sent down to South America also?

Blake: The Embassy reports. I remember no FBI reports.

Frank: In any case, they may have gone directly to FBI headquarters.

Blake: Oh, yes.

Frank: And you never got them anyway. Was there anything that stands out as being outstanding during your tour with ONI?

Blake: No, I don't think so, except it was a lot of fun.

Frank: Routine for the most part?

Blake: I would say so.

Frank: Any real flaps occur?

Blake: I imagine there were one or two. I don't remember the details of them.

Frank: Were you, as head of this Latin American desk, operating in a vacuum in the sense of what went on in the Far East? Were you pretty much concerned with your own bailiwick?

Blake: Yes, except that I used to drop in and see the other sections from time to time.

Frank: Was Zacharias there, for instance, at this time?

Blake: No. No, Zacharias was there when I was down at the Marine Corps Schools. I remember talking with him about Truk and what there might or might not be on Truk. I forget the name of the officer who was in charge.

Frank: Puleston was there at the time?

Blake: No. Puleston had been Director of Naval Intelligence. I remember very well Commander "Deke" Bridgett who came back from Japan where he'd been assistant naval attaché for air while I was in ONI. I'd known him from my days on the *Pennsylvania* when he was a j.g. I used to talk with him from time to time. After he'd been there about a month, he said, "You know, I came back from Japan all steamed up. I thought I had a message to give the people back here." He said, "It's all right here. I find every bit of it right here, and they just pay no attention." Well, there's not much that the military people can do under those circumstances, because they're subject to the policies of the civilian heads; and you can't keep running up to the President and the Secretary of State and getting them all steamed up about things

47

	they don't intend to get steamed up over. So you just have to wait and do the best you can.
Frank:	Were you aware at the time of any code breaking going on?
Blake:	Oh, yes.
Frank:	You knew about MAGIC and so on?
Blake:	I didn't know what the names were, but I knew they had a very successful code breaking operation going. As a matter of fact, I went in to see the officer in charge of it once. My secretary, who was Admiral Wilson's daughter, Eunice Wilson, had worked in that section at one time.
Frank:	Did you know Bill Eddy?
Blake:	I don't place him.
Frank:	He was a regular officer, I believe – a World War I officer – was expert in Arab affairs; as a matter of fact, was brought back and worked very closely there. He was president of Hobart College later.
Blake:	It rings no bell.
Frank:	Well, you then went to the War College in July of 1940.
Blake:	Yes.
Frank:	To be a student in the senior course.
Blake:	Yes.
Frank:	And in August you received your colonelcy.
Blake:	My outstanding recollection of the course at the War College was the operation against Truk, which was beaten off by aircraft before the attacking fleet even got within shooting range, showing that the Navy was very much alert to the use of aircraft in Naval warfare. Otherwise, they couldn't have used it so successfully right from the outset as they did.
Frank:	Even with the poor aircraft that it had.
Blake:	I had no knowledge that our naval aircraft at the outbreak of World War II were poor by the standards then existing.
Frank:	Now you said this commander came back there from Japan and all of you . . . Now, was ONI turned towards Japan primarily, or was it aware of possible involvement with Germany and Italy?
Blake:	Oh, yes, definitely. It did not wear blinders in any sense of the word. It was not specifically oriented in any direction. I would say that Europe and Asia were its major interests, which was quite natural.
Frank:	Did you feel that the senior course was worthwhile?
Blake:	Yes and no. I think it's very worthwhile for a Marine officer and just in a general Military cultural sense. But for any specific material used as a Marine officer, no. But it's well to be able to fit mentally into that picture and to know what's going on. It was in no sense of the word

time wasted. I think it's a valuable part of a senior Marine officer's education.

Frank: Was that a desirable assignment for a senior officer?

Blake: Well, they sent some very good officers there. General Geiger was in the class I was in, for instance. I think he was a lieutenant colonel then. No, he wasn't. He was a senior colonel.

Frank: He had to be a colonel.

Blake: Was he in that? No, he wasn't there. I thought I could see him in a picture that I had. But they always sent very representative Marine officers up there.

Frank: You then went on a tour of the chiefs of the Navy General Staff of the American republics. You were a guide then?

Blake: Each one of us was assigned a Latin American admiral – to be his aide, as it were, and his personal escort. I had the Chilean, Admiral J. Allard, a very fine gentleman.

Frank: We didn't talk about this goodwill cruise that you made while you were with ONI.

Blake: Oh, that was extremely interesting. We went to La Guaira and up to Caracas, of course; to Rio de Janeiro, Buenos Aires, through the Straits of Magellan, to Callao and Santiago, to Lima. I was just thinking how I got back home. I don't remember how I got back home. I left the ship at Balboa, I'm sure.

Frank: Were you assigned just as a guide or as an observer?

Blake: I think I went along primarily to act as interpreter for Admiral Kimmel.

Frank: That's before he went to Pearl Harbor.

Blake: Yes. He commanded the division of heavy cruisers. And the reason the trip was made at the request of the State Department, because the Italians had just made a similar cruise, and they wanted us to follow them up and counteract their influence.

Frank: Now, when you completed your instruction at the War College, you went down to Quantico to join the 5th Marines as commander; and then, of course, you were a guide down in Florida. The 1st Division had been formed in February at Guantanamo Bay. While at the War College, was there any emphasis placed or any instruction at all on amphibious warfare, amphibious assault landing?

Blake: I don't remember any. The Navy was still a very, very blue-water Navy. That died but died very slowly, and I'm not at all sure that it has died altogether. You'll remember Admiral Halsey went off chasing a fleet of Japanese vessels that weren't there and which he shouldn't have been chasing even if they were there because only an Act of God

	kept the Japanese fleet from getting into the transports and repulsing the invasion of the Philippines, you'll remember, and his job was to protect the transports.
Frank:	Your assignment as commander of an infantry regiment must have been a very choice assignment indeed.
Blake:	It was a very desirable assignment.
Frank:	And the 5th Marines, of course – your old outfit.
Blake:	Yes.
Frank:	You conducted training exercises and so on with them, is that correct?
Blake:	That's correct.
Frank:	And prepared generally for war. When did the reserves come in? Were they already on active duty?
Blake:	They were already on active duty.
Frank:	That's right. They'd been there. So you had quite a composite organization. Who were your battalion commanders, do you recall?
Blake:	General Edson, Bill Whalen and George Rowan.
Frank:	And your exec was who?
Blake:	Charlie Brooks.
Frank:	And who was your operations officer?
Blake:	I can't remember his name.
Frank:	The regiment moved from Quantico down to New River, which of course later became Lejeune. You moved down there in September '41 and were there when the war broke out. Had you been aware by '42 of the impending deployment overseas of the division as a whole?
Blake:	No.
Frank:	What was it like down at Lejeune when the division was formed? Hectic?
Blake:	Actually, Nicaragua was a much pleasanter place to live than the New River area at that time. They had mosquitoes there with snow on the ground.
Frank:	Things hadn't been fixed up yet.
Blake:	No.
Frank:	Your division commander at this time was Torrey, was it not?
Blake:	Yes.
Frank:	And, of course, the force commander was Smith. Who was Torrey's chief of staff – do you remember? Was Ellis Bell Miller there?
Blake:	Torrey's chief of staff? Roy Hunt.
Frank:	And who was it before him?
Blake:	I'm sure Hunt was the chief of staff when I joined the regiment, when I joined the division. I don't remember any other.

Frank: I was thinking of an earlier time when it was down in Cuba. When did General Vandegrift take over as division commander?

Blake: He relieved Torrey – I forget when that was.

(pause in recording)

Frank: We were talking about the 5th Marines, no longer the old 5th Regiment of World War I days. I believe they changed the designation in '32 or '31 of "regiments" to "Marines." It was the 5th Regiment till 1931, and then the designation was, a Marine Corps-wide redesignation to 5th Marines.

Blake: I really don't know. I don't remember. I didn't know whether that was an official designation or just the popular one.

Frank: Yes. In other words, it was 11th Marines instead of 11th Regiment. Now it was official. And at that time the number companies became letter. What was the division like at that time? Very active I think we said it was.

Blake: At Camp Lejeune?

Frank: Yes, sir.

Blake: Yes, it was training all the time.

Frank: Were you satisfied with the status of your regiment at this time? Were they measuring up?

Blake: Well, it was very difficult because there was a great deal of turnover.

Frank: Was it at this time that you lost Edson's battalion?

Blake: Yes. It became the 1st Raider Battalion, I think.

Frank: Yes. And did you have to give up any other troops to form other regiments?

Blake: I'm afraid I don't remember.

Frank: Most of the regiments were being hit pretty hard to form cadres for other units.

Blake: Yes, but specifically I couldn't say.

Frank: Of course war broke out while you were down at New River. I think the regiment was on pretty much of a war standing as it could be under the circumstances anyway.

Blake: I think so.

World War II 1942-1946

Frank: In April of '42 you were detached, which must have been somewhat of a wrench.

Blake: It was.

Frank: And then you went out to the Marine Corps base at San Diego . . .

Blake: And organized the 10th Defense Battalion.

Frank: Now, much has been said and written or at least a certain amount about the defense battalion concept, which I think was a product of Charlie Barrett's mind. I think it was he who originated it.

Blake: I really don't know.

Frank: With General Pepper, Lieutenant Colonel Pepper at the time. Of course, the 1st Defense Battalion – I think the first three were organized before the war began in '39. Now, you were not an artillery officer. Was there a requirement for a defense battalion to be commanded by an artillery officer?

Blake: No, or I wouldn't have been sent.[1]

Frank: Well, yes, that's true. But you had just prior to this been to the Naval War College. Had the advanced base concept been taught there?

Blake: Not that I remember. It was strictly fleet operations.

Frank: As I recall, the defense battalion was supposedly a tool or instrument or unit to be utilized in the advanced base operation.

Blake: That's my understanding, yes.

Frank: Also it seems to me that there were several different conformations of defense battalion organizations at this time. I think there were three or four different unit groupings. In other words, you'd have the 3-inch guns or the 3-inch anti-aircrafts or the 90mm.

Blake: Well, I think the 90mm became standard after it was developed. As a matter of fact, I don't remember having seen a 3-inch anti-aircraft with the defense battalion.

Frank: And then they had the coast artillery also.

Blake: They had the 155mm guns, yes.

Frank: Machine gun groupings?

Blake: Let's see: they had the 40mm . . . There were three units: 90mm, 155s, 40mm and the smaller one – what was that?

Frank: The 20mm?

[1] *But he had served two years as C.O. of the battleship Pennsylvania's Marine detachment, manning the ship's five-inch, 51 caliber guns. In June 1925 he received a commendation from the Chief of Naval Operations for achieving the highest score ever, with this type of gun.*

52

Blake:	Yes.
Frank:	Some defense battalion conformations also had a tank unit.
Blake:	Yes, we had I think six tanks.
Frank:	The defense battalion also was a very large organization.
Blake:	Well, in armament it was a composite artillery regiment. But because it was not mobile, its personnel were of battalion strength.
Frank:	Well, actually, I think the defense battalion personnel-wise was considerably larger than the normal infantry battalion.
Blake:	Oh, yes.
Frank:	The defense battalion would go to a thousand, 1100 or 1200 men, depending on groupings.
Blake:	Yes. Of course, with the advance of World War II, the tanks were removed from the defense battalions. There was no need for them.
Frank:	And finally the coast artillery was removed.
Blake:	The 155s? I don't know. I don't even know whether they have defense battalions now or not. I doubt it.
Frank:	No. But during the war, as a matter of fact, as the war bypassed the defense battalion and its use, they were redesignated Triple A battalions, anti-aircraft artillery battalions. I think it took place in '44, April of 1944. But it wasn't too long after you took over the 10th Defense Battalion before you left.
Blake:	Went out to Pearl Harbor, yes.
Frank:	And went from there to where?
Blake:	To the South Pacific, Purvis Bay on Florida Island. We were there for a little while, and then we went up to the Russell Islands. I went to the 3rd Division as chief of staff from there.
Frank:	You for a time were the anti-aircraft commander, artillery commander, and commander of the Marine defense group in the Solomon's. Was this while you were in the Russell's?
Blake:	Yes. Let me see . . .
Frank:	You had a temporary additional duty as commander Marine defense group in the Solomon's.
Blake:	Yes. I think I went down to Guadalcanal when I was given that designation. And then since it was all an area, I decided I could have my headquarters wherever I wanted to, so I went back to the 10th Defense Battalion.
Frank:	You took over chief of staff of the 3rd Division in August of '43. The 3rd Division was at that time in New Zealand?
Blake:	Guadalcanal.
Frank:	It had moved up from New Zealand already.
Blake:	Yes.

Frank:	And was getting ready for the Bougainville operation.
Blake:	Yes.
Frank:	The division commander was . . .
Blake:	Barrett.
Frank:	Barrett then went up to IMAC, I believe.
Blake:	And General Hal Turnage relieved him, and I became General Turnage's chief of staff.
Frank:	Was the division in pretty good shape at this time?
Blake:	I thought so.
Frank:	Combat ready in every respect?
Blake:	For all practical purposes.
Frank:	The Bougainville operation took place on the first of November, 1943, and you landed at Empress Augusta Bay. General Barrett had died, I believe – had he not?
Blake:	Yes.
Frank:	And Vandegrift had come back to take over IMAC (I Marine Amphibious Corps) and in essence supervise the overall Bougainville operation.
Blake:	Yes.
Frank:	How would you characterize the Bougainville operation?
Blake:	Well, it was miserable living because everything was so wet. It was very interesting soil there. Everything was swamp, but it was a sort of porous soil, and they could build roads by just going through the jungle with a drag line and scooping it up onto where they wanted the roadbed to be and level it off and they had a road. It drained right out. But until they got through the swampy ground particularly, it was very miserable. There was hard fighting. Only where the battalion landed on the beach where the airfield was to be built.
Frank:	Piva Strip.
Blake:	Yes.
Frank:	The Japanese mounted a counter landing, I believe.
Blake:	Oh, that was interesting. Nobody to this day knows how they got in there. They just went right by an occupied island; nobody shot at them; got in there and landed. John Bushrod Wilson's artillery battalion destroyed them.
Frank:	I think the 3rd Marines was put into the breach down there by the swamp, on the left of the creek there. Some of the inland fighting was quite interesting, was it not?

Tape 2, Side 2

| Blake: | The landing itself was mechanically difficult because there was quite a bit of surf, |

	And the coxswains were not as skillful as they might have been in keeping their boats from broaching. I've often wondered why the Navy didn't train their boats just in maneuvering for landing operations. Maybe they did, but I found no evidence of it if they did.

Frank: This was the second major Marine Corps landing in the Pacific, I believe. The first was Guadalcanal.

Blake: That's right. And, of course, Tarawa went on at the same time.

Frank: Yes. I think the landing there was about 13 November, 13 days later. Had the division's staff studied the lessons of Guadalcanal?

Blake: In what sense?

Frank: Well, going back to pre-World War II days, for instance, during the fleet landing exercises and when FTP-167 was used as a basis for the practice landings and the maneuvers, one of the greatest problems was the logistics problems – getting supplies off the beach. And essentially Guadalcanal was the first combat testing of amphibious warfare doctrine. So there had to be certain things that went well and certain things that went wrong, and certainly the supplies on the beach was something that was very bad at Guadalcanal. What I'm trying to determine is whether or not the way the 1st Division operated on Guadalcanal and what it did and didn't do, whether the report of the Guadalcanal operation figured in any way . . .

Blake: I never saw a report of the Guadalcanal operations. And so far as the handling and the accounting for supplies on the beach, that Guadalcanal problem lasted until the end of the war. They never did build up an adequate source for keeping track of supplies as they landed. And whether they have now or not, I wouldn't know.

Frank: I think the logistics train is so large then.

Blake: I tried to get it for the Island Command at Guam but didn't succeed. So, again, even the landing at Guam, the supplies came in catch as catch can.

Frank: The people who landed with the 3rd Division on Bougainville were mostly . . . This was the first operation for most of them.

Blake: Yes.

Frank: Except perhaps for your raiders and your para Marines?

Blake: I don't think any of them had been in a prior operation.

Frank: The division withdrew when – do you recall? I guess you went back in January of '44.

Blake: I don't remember when they were relieved.

Frank: But in any case you were given the 21st Marines in February of 1944.

Blake: Yes.

55

Frank:	Did you begin planning and training immediately?
Blake:	Yes.
Frank:	That operation was when?
Blake:	That never came off.
Frank:	Emirau?
Blake:	Where in the world was that to be?
Frank:	In the Admiralties?
Blake:	I just don't remember, but it didn't come off. Then I was sent to be chief of staff of the island command in Guam, for the Guam operation.
Frank:	You were Chief of Staff, V Amphibious Corps, or chief of staff . . .
Blake:	Of the Island Command.
Frank:	What did they call it? First Provisional Base Headquarters?
Blake:	I guess maybe it was. I don't know.
Frank:	You accompanied the invasion force?
Blake:	Yes.
Frank:	What was the composition of your island command?
Blake:	Oh, good Lord.
Frank:	Well, let me put it differently. What was the mission of your island command?
Blake:	To administer the island.
Frank:	Civilians and military?
Blake:	Yes. The military government was under the Island Command, the supply base, the Naval base; housekeeper for the occupying troops, as it were.
Frank:	Was that a very exciting or a very dull tour?
Blake:	No, it was interesting – to see that place develop. It had a very fine Seabee commander who did a terrific job there.
Frank:	And you had the Island Command until April of '45 or March of '45. You became deputy island commander. Who took over – Larsen?
Blake:	He was the island commander and I was his chief of staff. Then I was promoted to brigadier general, and they made me deputy island commander. What's-his-name came down from Tinian.
Frank:	Underhill?
Blake:	No, to be chief of staff. Doggie Arthur.
Frank:	You must have felt the war was passing you by to a considerable extent.
Blake:	It did.
Frank:	The assignment to the 10th Army then must have been somewhat more of a challenge and more interesting, or did you feel that?
Blake:	Well, I hoped it would be. But there was not much to do out there. The deputy chief of staff for Marines was just a liaison agent between

	the Marines and the 10th Army commander. General Stilwell was a magnificent person with whom to be associated, and I enjoyed that very much.
Frank:	Did you have anything to do, or were you closely involved with the buildup for the Operation OLYMPIC?
Blake:	No.
Frank:	Who had that responsibility on the island?
Blake:	As a matter of fact, I don't believe they had gotten around to it yet by the time the war was over.
Frank:	The 1st Division, of course, was still on the island, and so was the 2nd Wing.
Blake:	Yes.
Frank:	You left there in august of '45 for this occupation . . .
Blake:	I started home.
Frank:	You were on your way home?
Blake:	I got shanghaied at Guam to do down to Truk.
Frank:	Which one of your friends did that?
Blake:	I still don't know. I guess Henry Larsen thought it would be a good idea, and I didn't mind. I had nothing to go home to then.
Frank:	You worked under Admiral George Murray?
Blake:	ComMarianas.
Frank:	You took the surrender of Truk or did he?
Blake:	No, General Hermle went down for that.
Frank:	And where did you set up your headquarters? Your title, I believe, was the Commanding General Occupation Forces Truk and Central Carolinas.
Blake:	Something like that. I was on Truk, Dublon was the Japanese headquarters. I was on Moen where the Japanese airfield was which we expanded and improved.
Frank:	The idea was to build up the Naval operations base?
Blake:	My instructions were to establish a military government and evacuate the Japanese and build an airfield.
Frank:	You received, I think, a copy of the draft manuscript that I wrote on the return to the islands just about a year or year and a half ago. I think you commented on this.
Blake:	I don't remember.
Frank:	We have this down. This is written down up here.
Blake:	It's very interesting down there to see the damage we'd done. That place was just a wreck, just covered with shattered airplanes. The first thing we did was turn the Japanese to cleaning it up and dumping the material outside the reef. It was also very interesting to see the defenses

they had set up. Bypassing Truk was a very wise move. A tremendous barrier reef with the huge surf crashing down on it, and then these little islands on the reef, flanking the entrances, were of course well equipped with machine guns and light artillery. And the artillery on the islands inside the atoll were in caves that extended through the hill, so the guns stuck out over the lagoon; the entrances to the casemates were by tunnel from the defiladed side of the hill. They didn't have any really heavy guns. On the island that our headquarters was on they had I think it was two heavy cruiser turrets – they were 8-inch guns. That was the sum total of their heavy artillery. An interesting thing was that the Japanese command there was independent. We made our arrangements with the Army commander on the assumption that as the senior he was in command of the Navy, too, just as we had a unified operational command. And it worked out all right. But they did not have unified operational command any place so far as I know, and I think that detracted from the success of the Japanese war effort.

The Army, for instance, had all the supply of bug exterminator. So they had good sweet potato patches, and they were pretty well fed. But the Navy engineers' battalion were living skeletons. Their combat people they kept fed. But you'll find in the files someplace in Washington, if they haven't thrown them away, pictures that I sent in from Truk showing these Japanese construction battalion men looking just like skeletons with the skin tautly drawn over them.

Frank: I've seen those pictures.

Blake: I sent in quite detailed reports on Truk Island.

Frank: I forget who had the battalion, surrender battalion. [Note: Sparlock] He sent in pictures of you inspecting. How about war crimes? Wasn't this one of your missions, to seek out war criminals and evidence of war crime?

Blake: I don't remember having received any instructions on that, but we did have an officer assigned to it. They dug up some stuff there. There were some executions of American prisoners, and we found who the guilty were and they were brought to trial. Vice Admiral Hara was tried. He was sentenced for four or five years to prison, something like that. Now, what happened to the warrant officer who did the executing, I don't know.

Frank: There were a number of executions at Guam. I think there was a BQO – a block stockade for enemy POWs. Anything that sticks out in your mind from this particular tour of duty?

Blake: No, I don't think so, except the Seabee battalion they sent me was an awful outfit. They were all relatively inexperienced men. They all wanted to go home; their officers didn't care. After the Seabee battalions that I had seen and been working with during the war, it was quite a shock. Finally the construction officer on the staff of ComMarianas came down, and the bulk of the work was turned over to the Japanese.

Frank: The Japanese were rather cooperative after they surrendered, were they not?

Blake: Completely and totally.

Frank: You wondered if they were the same people that we fought.

Blake: Well, they were well disciplined.

Down-sizing after the War 1946-49

Frank: You next went back to Headquarters and became president of the Marine Corps Post War Reorganization Board and president of the Naval Retirement Board. Exactly what was this board, because it met for quite a while, I see?

Blake: It studied the records of all the officers who wanted to stay in the service and made recommendations on the basis of the records.

Frank: Was this both regular and reserve or just reserve?

Blake: No, it was just for the regular Marine Corps, as I remember it.

Frank: This had nothing to do with the integration of the reserves?

Blake: This was for officers for duty with the regular commissioned officers. I imagine there were reservists on it – I don't remember. Probably most of them were reserves.

Frank: Reserves who wanted to stay in the Marine Corps. Did the Marine Corps get as many people as it wanted for this program?

Blake: My recollection is, yes.

Frank: In other words, the board could keep high standards.

Blake: Yes, and I think did.

Frank: In October of '46 you became the Inspector General of the Marine Corps. Were you the first one?

Blake: No, General del Valle was. He went to Personnel, and I relieved him.

Frank: This must have been quite a busy time.

Blake: Oh, there was a lot of inspecting to do.

Frank: What did you find on your inspection trips? How did you find the state of the Marine Corps?

Blake: Very good by and large – much, much better than after World War I, believe me.

Frank: Morale was high?

Blake: Yes, and standards were high.

Frank: Did this rapid demobilization have a serious effect on the state of the Corps?

Blake: As I remember, no. It limited its capacity, of course, but I don't think it was serious. The surprising thing to me was that it didn't seem to affect the quality of what was left.

Frank: Well, in the more complex specialties – the aviators, aviation mechanics and so on – did the loss of many of the trained men affect their mission?

Blake: It may have. I don't know.

Frank: Did you get out to China at all?

Blake: Yes.

Frank: And what did you find out there?

Blake: Tsingtao was the only place we had Marines. That was in fine shape.
            They had a little trouble with an urgent plumbing requisition that got
            lost. My good friend General Watson worked me over just because I
            was from headquarters as I went through Pearl Harbor, but it was found
            at the bottom of a G-4's basket. The quartermaster general, when the
            radio was received inquiring concerning the requisition, didn't bother
            to look beyond his own files. Being for special supplies, the requisition
            had required the commandant's approval and been routed to G-4, not
            to OMG. I could never convince Pete Hill that the staff was lacking
            grossly in a sense of intellectual curiosity, because when I got back I
            found out where it was in three minutes. I called up Central files. But,
            you see, the quartermaster keeps his own private files, and anything
            that comes in concerning quartermaster problems, he just goes to his
            file – he won't go anyplace else. So I called up central files and they
            told me exactly where it had gone, and I went there and I found it
            – and then Jerry Thomas's plumbing went on its way.

Frank: He was out at Tsingtao as CG, FMFWesPac.
            I notice that you went in October of '47 – 1-8 October – on temporary
            duty to Pacific Ocean Areas in connection with a special investigation.
            Do you recall the circumstances of that?

Blake: I think that must have been on connection with a handling of rations
            by Van Orden. It was a peculiarly worded order. I absolved him of all
            blame, because he did what the letter of the order said. But both the
            quartermaster and chief of the department of personnel overruled me,
            because that wasn't what the order meant. I said, "Well, how in the
            world would George Van Orden know what the order meant? This is
            what it said." But he got a letter of reprimand out of it. It had something
            to do with rations – I forget what it was – but as far as I was concerned,
            he was carrying out the letter of the order, precisely what it said.

Frank: It seems to me that if the decision of the inspector general makes as a
            result of an investigation is to be overruled by other staff agencies at
            headquarters, the inspector general is just a figurehead and he might as
            well not be.

Blake: Well, we've got the track back to the Commandant. [The IG had a
            direct line of communication open to the Commandant.]

Frank: And the Commandant went ahead with what the quartermaster and
            director of personnel had to say?

Blake: Yes.

Frank: Well, we'll let that speak for itself. I might say that the Director of Personnel was del Valle at the time; the quartermaster was W.P.T. Hill – both of them old friends of General Vandegrift.

Blake: And mine, too.

Frank: Yes, you all go back to the same time. I don't know: from an objective point of view at this stage of the game, it seems to me that the inspector general's say-so in a matter such as this should have carried more weight, since he was on the scene and investigated it.

Blake: Well, I felt that the order should have been written to say what they mean. And even if it might be obvious to the person carrying it out that they meant something else and he was taking advantage of a poorly worded order, I felt that the fact that he did what the order said justified what he did – because when you start trying to interpret orders, then the whole system is in trouble.

Frank: You were quite busy on board at this time. Now, did the promotion board – the board to select lieutenant colonels for promotion to colonel – was that a standing board? Because here you're on it in December of '46, January of '47, February, March, April, May, June of '47, July of '47, August – right through there, as a matter of fact, for almost two years.

Blake: I don't remember quite frankly.

Frank: You were also a member of the board to hear cases of officers of the United States Marine Corps, Marine Corps Reserve, revocation of whose commissions had been recommended. Now, do these individuals include both former enlisted men as well as those who were to be reverted down a grade or two?

Blake: I would presume so, but again I don't remember. That's 20 years ago.

Frank: These appear to have been standing boards, standing committees. You went out to Tsingtao in October of '47, I believe it was. No, in June of '48 was when you made the trip – that's when General Thomas had FMF WesPac. There seems to have been considerable ferment after the war in the Marine Corps of changes, as we spoke of before – different assignments, the redesignation of units, disbandment of other units. Of course, of all the wartime divisions, only two were in existence at this time – the 1st and the 2nd, plus I think you had a 1st Brigade on Guam. That may have come a little later.

Blake: The 1st Brigade on Guam – I inspected them out there.

Frank: General Craig had that.

Blake: General Craig had it. He went from there to Korea, I think.

Frank: The brigade was brought back to the west coast, I believe, when the 1st Division came back. Now, you remained as inspector . . . [tape went bad here] . . . of Japan. Was there anything that you were particularly unhappy about when you were the inspector general?

[something goes very wrong with the recording here]

Before we had a stop for repairs, General, we were talking about the board and the people who wanted to integrate. We talked about the condition of the Corps. You were comparing them with the immediate post-World War I days.

Blake: I found it very superior.

Frank: You served under two Commandants as inspector general, both Cates and Vandegrift. We were also talking about the integration fight at this time, which was a very difficult period for the Marine Corps.

Blake: Well, I don't know whether it was very difficult for the Marine Corps or not, because Congress was very much on our side. General Vandegrift and a Navy aviator, Crommelin, had been fighting integration; and so far as I could see – I may be very, very wrong on this – the Navy as a whole, although it did not like it, somehow or other seemed paralyzed and wasn't doing anything. And General Vandegrift, also Cliff Cates, was carrying the burden of the fight. And then an element developed that wanted to bargain the Marine Corps off against Navy independence. General Vandegrift called the general officers on duty at Headquarters Marine Corps in a conference, explained to them the situation, and said that he was now giving up on the Navy fight, and he was dedicating himself to assuring the future of the Marine Corps, which he did very successfully.

Frank: If my information is correct, at that conference he asked the Marine Corps general officers there present to assist in any means possible, if they had any political influence or anything up on the Hill, to employ that influence, employ their associations with the legislators to support the Marine Corps program, to get them to help out.

Blake: I don't remember that specifically, but it is very reasonable to believe that he did say it.

Frank: Now, to your knowledge was there wholehearted cooperation? Did all Marine Corps general officers who were asked to do so get involved?

Blake: I'm sure all who had any contacts did. I didn't have any contacts that I could approach on the subject.

Frank: During this period, the time that you were Inspector General of the Marine Corps found going the way, the path pretty difficult under the Johnson regime – Secretary of Defense Louis Johnson – did it not?

Blake: I don't remember. I don't believe anything of that nature came to my attention. As a matter of fact, I remember very little about the Johnson

63

regime except that he did a lot of cutting back, didn't he, that had to be undone?

Frank: Yes, well, on your inspection trips did you find that the tight fiscal regime of the Marine Corps affected the mission and affected the role that existing units could play?

Blake: Not within what I saw or not within what my mission was. Naturally, limited funds would limit the expenditures that could be put on training, limit what the Marine Corps could do, limit the size of the Marine Corps – but beyond that, I don't remember having noted anything.

Frank: Well, General, in a period of about five hours, we've covered approximately 32 years of a very filled and very interesting Marine Corps career.

Blake: Well, I think all Marine Corps careers are interesting.

Frank: I know that you've been reticent to talk about yourself in certain areas.

Blake: I have no complaints to make.

Frank: I'm not talking about any heartburn on your part, but I mean things that you've played a decided role in – that you've just in the course of conversation downplayed or have not spoken about to the extent that perhaps you wanted to or could. What would you say are your most outstanding memories in these 32 years?

Blake: Well, of course, there's a comradeship. There's no closer comradeship than the comradeship of arms. And the drama, the drama of battle, and the loneliness of the battlefield. Ever since the machine gun was invented, everything that's seen on the battlefield is dead or pretty close to it. I'll never forget the morning of the landing at Guam. When night fell we were alone on the ocean. When dawn broke, as far as the eye could see over the horizon, there was a mass of ships – a tremendous sight. And I've often thought: What did the Japanese think on Guam when they saw that huge invasion force? And then the lazy boom and explosion of the Naval bombardment. I couldn't help but compare it to the preparatory bombardment the morning of November 1st, 1918 – that tremendous sound. And when they reached their objective at Soissons, the 1st Moroccan Division was on our left and the line bent back; and the 1st Division beyond the Moroccans resumed the attack. We were sitting right there on the cross section of it. There were the fleeing Germans; there was the rolling barrage, and behind the barrage came the 1st Division infantry. It was a beautiful sight. I don't think things like that will ever be seen again because warfare has changed. In those days we couldn't mass men because the machine gun had stopped that. Now you have to move men in even smaller units.

Frank: Of all your associations during your 32 years in the Marine Corps, who stands out as being most memorable?

Blake: Well, that's very difficult. That's very difficult. Louie Cukela was probably the most fantastic.

Frank: Really? Where did you know him?

Blake: France.

Frank: Was he in your company?

Blake: Yes. He got the Medal of Honor for his action in Soissons, and he was first awarded the Distinguished Service Cross. I was in the 17th Company then; he was in the 66th. After I came back from the hospital, I was given the 66th Company. So when the war was over, General Lejeune sent a letter down to the company saying that in reading over Captain Cukela's citation for the Distinguished Service Cross, he felt that it merited a higher award and asked if we wouldn't resubmit it for a Medal of Honor. So I called various men in the company who had been there to question them about it, and the first one came in. He said, "Captain Cukela didn't do that at all." He said, "I did it." Well, I called another one in, and he said, "Captain Cukela was just terrific, just terrific. Here we were pinned down, couldn't move; you couldn't even wiggle an eyebrow. And then along through the woods came Louie Cukela pushing the bullets to the right and the left." His written statement became a little less dramatic than that, but it went through; and there was no doubt that he was a tremendous Marine who was spoiled by having been made an officer.

Frank: I was going to ask you that – did having been made an officer spoil him?

Blake: Oh, yes; oh, yes.

Frank: He fancied himself as something of a character thereafter.

Blake: Yes. There were all his fantastic remarks such as "If I want to send a goddamned fool, I'd go myself," when a messenger came back with a stupid garbled reply.

Frank: I heard that.

Blake: But so far as outstanding officers are concerned, it's very hard to pick and choose. I would hate to pick anyone specifically. Of course, I think General Vandegrift was particularly outstanding for his moral courage. It took a lot of doing at Guadalcanal, and if he ever felt let down, no one else ever knew it.

    Roy Hunt was a magnificent troop leader, perhaps the best. He had a tremendous faculty for attracting the loyalty and confidence of his men. And when you have that, confidence doesn't make much difference.

Then Oliver Smith was good at anything. I feel that his great feat was the fight back to the sea from the Chosin Reservoir against, I have read, five Chinese divisions. That was one of the most outstanding feats of arms in the history of warfare. This one division, this one division, was the only fighting unit left in Korea in the whole American Army so far as I can see. When we were living in Santa Barbara, the city brought down a group of Korean wounded from the hospitals to attend their annual post-Spanish days fiesta, which was a very colorful thing. I was talking with one of the men who was in with General Smith in Korea. He said, "I'd follow him to hell because I know he'd get me out."

Frank: I imagine there was some question when he was eligible to become commandant and he didn't become commandant.

Blake: Well, he would have made a wonderful commandant. I'd never heard him mentioned for commandant, although he would have been my choice; but there were so many good ones – just like the present fight for commandant. It was hard to go wrong so far as a competent choice was concerned.

Frank: Did you know all three choices last time?

Blake: I'm not sure that I remembered any of them, although perhaps I might well have served with them. Of course, my choice is Jim Masters. I think he's a very remarkable officer. And so is his young brother, Bud. But Jim Masters, as far as I'm concerned, is tops.

Frank: Well, sir, we've talked about everything under the sun as far as the Marine Corps is concerned. I want to thank you very much.

Blake: Well, I don't know whether I've contributed anything that may have been worthwhile. It may have been helpful in a spot or two.

Frank: Well, I'm sure that when you get the transcript, some things may come to mind, and you can probably add them.

Blake: The commander at the Marianas under whom I served at Truk was Vice-Admiral George C. Murray.

Frank: Well, as General Chapman's representative from the Historical Branch, Headquarters, I want to thank you very much for your cooperation and time.

Blake: It's been a pleasure. I hope I've given you something of value, although I doubt it.

Frank: Well, you're being modest. Thank you again.

End

Fig. 1 C.O. and officers of the 66th Company , France 1918

Fig. 2 Provost Marshal , Quantico, 1921

Fig. 3 Captain 's Inspection for War Secretary Henry Stimson , Goat Island , 1927.

Fig. 4   With Captain Pete Geyer and unidentified Marine on the Coco River, Nicaragua ,
1928

Fig. 5   In mufti in Sevilla , Spain , 1931

Fig. 6   Major Blake (center) and Marine staff for the Nicaraguan National Board of
Elections , 1932

Fig. 7   Lt. Col. Blake (third from left) with RADM Yancey Williams , Cuba , 1937

Fig. 8   In Argentine Presidential Palace , Buenos Aires , on CRUDIV 7 Latin-America
goodwill cruise , 1939. Center, RADM Husband Kimmel;
Lt. Col. Blake, second from left.

Fig. 9 Col. Blake as C.O. 5th Marines , New River NC , 1941

Fig. 10 Col . Blake (in helmet) as C.O. 21st Marines , with Major General Alan H. Turnage , Guadalcanal 1944.

Fig. 11 Brig. General Blake (right) with Japanese Vice Admiral Hara and interpreters , Truk, 1945

Fig. 12 Commanding General Occupation Forces, Truk and Central Carolines, and staff, Moen Island, Truk Atoll , 1946

Robert Wallace Blake

Part II

The Travel Journal of Rosselet Wallace Blake

Robert Wallace Blake

Introduction

My mother, Rosselet Alice Wallace, was a Native Daughter of the Golden West, born in San Francisco in 1895. She was named for her two grandmothers, Rosselet Wallace, a native of Switzerland, and Alice Neiman, born in Pennsylvania. She was the oldest of four girls, the only one born in San Francisco. The family moved to Alameda shortly after Rosselet was born, and then to Berkeley, where all the girls grew up.

My grandmother was a Christian Scientist and the children were brought up in that faith. Rosselet was a devout Scientist her whole life.

The Berkeley public schools in that era were excellent, and the Wallaces were believers in public education. Rosselet and her sisters were all products of the Berkeley school system and went on to graduate from the University of California. Rosselet majored in English, with a minor in French, and qualified for her teaching certificate while an undergraduate.

She graduated from the University in May, 1917. The U.S. was at war with Germany. Rosselet wanted to do her part, so she got a job with the Department of Labor and took the train to Washington, DC. She was still there in 1919 after the war ended.

Rosselet Wallace and Robert Blake met when they both attended Whittier School in Berkeley. They were classmates at Berkeley High and the University. They were close but not engaged when World War I came and Robert went to France in the Marines, but they exchanged letters regularly all the time he was away. When Robert returned from Germany in July 1919, he received orders back to California but Rosselet was not there. At Christmas, he took leave to visit her, then wangled a set of orders to Quantico, just 40 miles from Washington. Sometime in the spring of 1920 they became engaged. Rosselet went home to prepare for the wedding. In July, Robert took leave to join her in Berkeley. They were married at the Wallace home where Rosselet had lived since she was eleven. The rest of this story is a narrative of Rosselet and Robert's travels together after that, most of it in Rosselet's own words.

Commentary between journal entries and footnotes to the journal are by this writer.

Robert Wallace Blake

Robert and Rosselet Blake in travelling attire after their wedding. Berkeley CA, June 30, 1920.

Chapter 1

Travels 1920 – 1931

Rosselet Blake's first journey as a Marine officer's wife was her honeymoon. She and Robert took the train from Berkeley CA to Quantico VA.

They made the customary stops at Lake Louise, Banff, and Niagara Falls, and visited in Hamilton, Ontario, with Robert's Canadian cousins. In Quantico, the following year a son was born. The year after that came the first separation, with Captain Blake detached from Quantico for a five-months cruise to the Far East with the Secretary of the Navy, an official visit to Japan and China. Rosselet took her ten-month-old baby on the Overland Limited to visit her mother and father in Berkeley.

In September 1922 Robert returned from the Far East with orders to the Mare Island CA Navy Yard. Rosselet joined him there, in a rose-covered bungalow labeled Quarters #6.[2] Seven months later came another tour of sea duty, with Robert assigned as C.O. of the Marine detachment of the battleship Pennsylvania.

My mother later described her next two years as "living like a sailor's girlfriend" as she followed the Pacific fleet from port to port up and down the Pacific Coats between San Pedro and Seattle. When the fleet finally took off for a new permanent base in Honolulu, Rosselet stayed in Seattle.

In May 1925 the Blakes were back in Mare Island, this time in Quarters #7. This time they only stayed six months, when Robert received new orders to command the Marine Detachment at the Naval Receiving Station, Goat Island, in the middle of San Francisco Bay. In those days Goat Island was only accessible by ferry. For the next four years Blake family travel was mostly by ferry, commuter rail, and streetcar. They did not own a car. The summer of 1927 Robert and Rosselet took a pack trip in the High Sierras by mule train on a Sierra Club excursion. Young Robert stayed with his grandparents.

Six months later came another separation when Robert received orders to Nicaragua, to a hill station where families were not allowed. Rosselet and son remained in Berkeley. This separation was to last eighteen months. In the summer of 1929, the Marine 11th Regiment was withdrawn from Nicaragua, with orders to Quantico. The Navy transport Henderson sailed down from San Francisco to Corinto to pick them up, families on board. From Corinto we all steamed through the Panama Canal, stopped once at Port-au-Prince, north to Chesapeake Bay, and

---

[2]A photo in the family album shows it clearly covered with roses.

up the Potomac River, to dock at the Quantico Pier. The Blake family would only be together in Quantico for a year.

In the summer of 1930 Captain Blake received orders for a second tour in Nicaragua, this time to safeguard the elections of the coming fall. Again, families would not be allowed, but this time Nicaragua "widows" were allowed to stay in their Quantico quarters. We now had a car, a new DeSoto coupe with a rumble seat, so we could get around the post with my father away.

The election detail ended in November. My father returned, not to Quantico, but to USMC Headquarters in Washington. My parents found a row house to rent in Washington's Berlieth district, an easy commute. But we were not to stay long. Early in March 1931, my father received a letter of advance information which read in its entirety:

> It is the present intention of the Major General Commandant to order you to Madrid, Spain, about April 1931, for duty and instruction in Spanish. The cost of tuition will be born by you.[3]

And so began an adventure which Rosselet Blake henceforth relates in her journal.

---

[3]*Letter from Major General Commandant, dated March 13, 1931.*

Chapter 2

A Year in Spain

April 11, 1931 – New York City – departure

Here we are, aboard the *George Washington*,[4] about to set sail for Spain. The ship sails at 10:30 P.M. It is dark. All that we can see of New York is the brilliantly lighted windows of the towering buildings. They are like golden checkerboards in great dark oblongs. It does not seem true—it cannot be real that we are going to Europe.

We left Washington in the early afternoon—Captain Walsh kindly took us to the train. The whole family were most thoughtful—feeding us and looking after us on our flurry of departure. I shall never forget Juanita's bountiful hospitality. When we reached New York and the Pennsylvania Hotel we decided to go immediately to the ship so took a taxi and went aboard. We put Bobby to bed almost immediately Found a beautiful mammoth tin box of sweets from Papa and several telegrams, steamer letters and books.

Robert and I walked about the ship to explore our new home. On deck we gazed at the skyline—Then went below to the nice writing room to write a letter. Suddenly I heard Ethel Edson's[5] voice and turned to find that the Edsons had driven up from Philadelphia to say goodbye to us. What dears they are! How I wish that they were going with us! They went ashore about ten. Then as we were tired we retired, too exhausted to see the *George Washington* glide past the Statue of Liberty.

In voyage

There are some pleasant English people at our table—the Lamonts. He owns a glass factory. They have been visiting in Oakland, California—How near home! The majority of passengers are Army officers and their wives going to Paris to prepare for the Gold Star Mothers' Pilgrimage. With us are Captain-Mrs. Blythe Jones and Wayne.

We kept a great deal to ourselves—I was tired—and spent practically all the time reading and resting. There was not much gaiety—only one or two dances after dinner.

Fine weather the first three days, then passed through a squall, but the following three days were fine again.

Arrived at Plymouth England Sunday morning about ten o'clock. The shore looked remarkably like the California shore line, brown hills, cliffs very much like the approach to San Francisco. It seemed thrilling after a week at sea. Reached Cherbourg about two o'clock at night but spent the night aboard being awakened

---

[4]*The same ship that carried President Wilson to France for the Paris Peace Conference, and brought home the Marine 5th Regiment after World War I.*
[5]*Wife of Captain Merritt Edson (later Brigadier General), USMC*

at four o'clock in the morning to go ashore. But after breakfast and all preparations were made had to wait several hours before we could go aboard the lighter. It was foggy and cold. Cherbourg is a quaint old town, with Normany houses along the waterfront. After going through the customs took the train for Paris where we arrived at 2 PM, after the most delightful ride through green spring time landscape past quaint farms and many lovely chateaux.

We all filed hungrily into the diner when call to lunch was issued—We marveled at the delicious food—It was served from large platters and passed to everyone. Each helped himself to whatever amount he craved. Then it was passed again for seconds. Soon the platter of ice-cream was passed twice. It was a table d'hote dinner. Everyone had the same thing. There were wines and vichy water. Robert enjoyed the former and we relished the latter.

Our compartment companion was an unusual looking and attractive French girl. She said that she was returning from a year in America.

Leontine[6] and Fernand in uniform met us and piloted us with our companions the Jones to Madame Dessarts' pension 5 rue Honoré Chevalier in the Latin Quarter just a half block from the Luxembourg Gardens. It was good to be with Leontine.

Madame Dessart gave us rooms belonging to some ladies who are visiting in Spain. She has an old house—one of the oldest in the quarter on the bend of a short little street. She serves plain food, but it is well prepared—savory—and tastes good. Her pension is full—several Americans—but the majority are French. Madame Dessart herself occupies her "salon" at night and in the morning often is found in a nightcap sitting up in bed shelling peas in the grandeur of the "salon".

At meal times Madame sits at the head of one of the long tables surrounded by those she considers the most "ranky."

Paris France. April 21st – 28th, 1931 -- and on to Spain

This morning dawned clear and sunny. We cannot but marvel at the trees in leaf, the advanced state of spring, when we left Washington only a week ago in the midst of winter.

Thursday we visited Notre Dame—walking from the pension through the Luxembourg Gardens—and their lacey greenery—spotted with sunshine, past some side walk cafés of the Latin Quarter—past the Red Mill and finally out across the boulevard and bridge to the cathedral. It was beautiful. Robert took some photographs. It is grey and Gothic and lovely inside—rather dark but the arches and beautiful colorings and Bible scenes in the stained glass windows made us stand and admire. We also visited St. Chapelle—an exquisite little church where the royal families worshipped—with the most intricate and exquisite gold and colored art work in the panellings.

In the afternoon to the Invalides—Napoleon's tomb, the Place de la Concorde and the Madeleine. Everyone writes of these—there is little that is new to say—but

---

[6]*Leontine Wallace, my mother's sister, then engaged to a French Army Lieutenant.*

it's always interesting. Of course Napoleon's tomb is fine but not touching and beautiful as the churches are. Of course Napoleon never has been much of an inspiration; he was too ruthless, too much of an egoist.

In the morning a tour of the Montparnasse.

Interesting but a little depressing. All the crowded brightly lighted cafés—filled with students had a very crude aspect—they looked tawdry—unromantic, a bit down at the heels. I was shocked to feel this way. However the students appeared to be enjoying themselves. With the exception of a number—girls highly made up, a bit cheap looking—They looked tired and disillusioned. Some were American girls—The poor student's life in Paris is far from romantic—it is plain bread and butter and very little of that. The poverty stood out starkly.

Wednesday we visited the famous paintings in the Louvre. It was a wonderful feast, Leontine selecting only the best known among the miles and miles of gallerys. Then out to the Tuilleries gardens with the fountains playing in the sunshine.

And on to the shopping district where we visited several department stores and a handkerchief shop. I bought a hat and Lois[7] some handkerschiefs. And had tea in an English book shop. In the evening had a little party at home in our room.

Robert and the Jones left in the morning for Madrid. We had tea in the afternoon with Mrs. Dulley and her mother Mrs Jackson, two charming American ladies—Mrs Dulley is attending the Sorbonne,

Visited an art exhibit at Les Independents—Leontine's work was most promising and hung in a favorite place next to André Lhôte's![8]

Visited the Bois de Boulogne—where a sudden shower caught us—but it was gone as rapidly as it appeared, and we walked back through the woods to the Arc de Triomphe and the Unknown Soldier's Tomb. A most impressive place, for the Arc is the center of all the avenues and boulevards which radiate from it spokewise.

Enjoyed going to church in the Trocadero. And the view of the Eiffel tower.

We left Paris on the luxurious Sud Express—few people traveling. In our car only two men—one was a french modiste from Madrid who had made clothes for the Infantas of the King of Spain and had made a hurried trip to Paris with some gowns unfinished before their hurried flight a few weeks ago. He told me his story in French. He had a beautiful ruby stick pin from the Queen and the signed photograph of the Infantas—all of which he displayed with much pride. We are going to a Republic instead of a kingdom—for King Alfonso left the throne as we were crossing the Atlantic.

We passed through Joan of Arc's town and the South of France in the late afternoon.[9] In the morning as we awakened about six o'clock we were hurrying

---

[7]*Mrs. Blythe Jones.*
[8]*French painter and painting teacher, 1885 – c. 1970*
[9]*At Hendaye in France we crossed the border and changed to a Spanish train on wider tracks (to prevent another Napoleonic force taking an army directly into Spain).*

along after our large fine engine with its little whistle which sounded like a peanut vendor's whistle or one they had at one time on the Merry-Go-Round in Golden Gate Park. It was bright and sunny—the rosy glow of sunrise was still on the horizon—the country was barren—an endless desert with occasional low flat villages of yellow sandstone. Soon a dream appeared. It was a medieval walled town—right out of a fairy book; all golden in the morning light. There was an almost square city built on a hill with walls ascending the heights. The walls were waving thick and turretted. It was Avila. A few hours later we descended at Madrid. Robert met us and escorted us to our pension—the Romero.

What a clamor and confusion there is in European cities! We are on the 5th floor, but the harsh ringing of a traffic bell on the street below—and the incessant honk-honk of the taxis and the street cars and clamor of the crowds drifts upward all day and all night There is quiet between the hours of two and five—Then we hear the clatter of donkeys hoofs—the voices of vendors and the noise and bustle of the street cleaners as they give the thoroughfares their morning bath from the fire hose. And we are in Madrid on the Gran Via.

Gran Via from the balcony of the Pension Romero. Madrid . 1931.

May 10th – 1931 – Segovia

The Spanish Labor Day—*Dos de Mayo* was interesting. We were awakened early in the morning by the *gente* in the streets, singing and dancing and laughing as they went on their way to the *campo*, with their lunches, to spend the day outside the city and to make merry—a Spanish holiday.

But today, we too, went to the country. And in addition, to an ancient city where even the early Phoenicians found a settlement years ago—Segovia, perhaps the most charming city in Spain.

We left Madrid at eight o'clock Sunday morning and arrived in Segovia about eleven. On our way we ascended the Guadarrama mountains, slowly winding our way upward until we saw a fine sanatorium high up on the mountainside—when we suddenly entered a tunnel—and were on the other side.

A bus convoyed us from the Station on the plain at Segovia through the winding hilly streets, narrowed and cobblestoned of course, under the arches of the Roman Aqueduct, through the Plaza and down a narrow winding street to the Commercio Hotel. A most satisfactory hostelry—old fashioned—Spanish—with large rooms but water pitcher for ablutions—and spittoons on the landings of the stairway.

However the food was excellent—well cooked meats and nicely prepared vegetables. The best we had tasted so far excepting the occasional but excellent meals we had at the Hotel Nacional in Madrid. Pension Romero is friendly with its small clientele—Everyone speaks as we enter the dining room—"*Que le aproveche*" they say which means "may you enjoy your dinner"—more or less. But to state that we do enjoy our dinner would be optimistic—bold overstatement. They are quite to be forgotten. Hence the warmth with which we greeted the fine asparagus in the Commercio.

We took a walk in the afternoon visiting the Alcázar a dramatic old castle built on the sheer cliffs at the edge of the town. From the point in the river viewed from the road on the opposite bank it does look like the prow of a ship—rising—thrillingly above the placid waters in the two small rivers. Here the Kings of Spain lived for five hundred years. Here Queen Isabella was married to Ferdinand. A moat protects the side where no rivers flow. But it is only the exterior which is old. Inside it has been rebuilt for it was destroyed by fire. Nevertheless the interior of ancient times has been reproduced. All castles without furniture and tapestries are gloomy. They seem more like prisons. In one of the tall medieval towers there are dungeons where prisoners were kept. Robert and Bobby ascended the winding staircase to the roof.

We met a party of Americans going through the Alcázar when we were admiring Isabella's throne room. To a foreigner who speaks not a word of this latin language it was good to hear English. One of the girls was studying at the University of Madrid. We plan to see something of her on our return.

85

Later, we descended many steps and crossed the river, which is bordered by green luxuriant looking vegetable gardens. Then ambled down a winding road—always looking at the picturesque town on the hills across the river with its stone houses clinging to the sides of the hills—the red thatched roofs, the geranium pots on the balconies. And the *piéce de resistance*—the finest view of all—when we reached the little cluster of trees at the junction in the river and gazed upward at the Alcázar.

The Alcázar , Segovia, 1931.

A fine view of the Guadarramas about forty miles away is had from a high point on a winding street. Here we stopped at a café so that we might sit at an out of door table and admire the view of the snow capped peaks.

The following day we visited the lovely Cathedral—a gem in sandstone—and the great Aqueduct—made from great blocks of stone piled upon one another without mortar or any material to hold them together. At its greatest height it reaches one hundred feet. Its arches are still intact. It still brings water from the far off Guadarramas.

We looked for living quarters in case we should settle here. It was difficult to find anything with conveniences such as heat and modern plumbing. We did find a very attractive and artistic apartment house built on the hillside—with lovely views—but baths in only one or two apartments—I saw no heat in any house. Many of them were very old, musty and smelly. In the older ones the bedrooms had no windows.

An American artist and his wife are living at our hotel. It would be a pleasant place to live.

We left at five o'clock and reached Madrid at eight. We smelled smoke and saw fires as we approached Madrid. In the city it was very dense and we drove home to find that a convent a short distance from our pension, with a number of other convents, had been harmed. The communists, the anti-jesuit group and who knows who else. Riots, in the Puerta del Sol that night. It was a very dramatic ending to a quiet expedition into old Spain. The new republic is in the throes of birth.

July 6, 1931 <u>Toledo</u> – Spain

It was a happy experience to be journeying out from Madrid this morning with Mamma, Papa and Leontine.[10] We caught a glimpse of the great monastery of Philip the second—the Escorial as we went by in the train. Toledo too is built on a hill and one approaches it from a railway station on a plain by means of winding climbing streets. We engaged a car in which we drove around the town obtaining a fine view of its lofty location and walls and old bridges. A city of countless civilizations—the capital of the Gothic Kings. I shall always remember the exquisite little Jewish synagogue—the more ponderous Arabic Santa Maria La Blanca—and the Catholic cathedral. Of course the latter is the real object of interest in Toledo for most travelers. It was the seat of the Archbishop of Spain—the richest cathedral in Spain. Small wonder that Ibañez's great novel, to the Spaniard, is *The Cathedral*.

Here we spent that entire afternoon. Our guide took us about to all the other points of interest in the morning ending up with the visit to El Greco's beautiful home—a low rambling stucco house with tiled roof and patio and garden—iron grills—charming old tiled fireplace and all the artistic decorations which we expect in a perfect Spanish house. It was a spot in which to rest and think of all that El Greco means. It was a house to carry with one in one's dreams—and perhaps to build someday[11]—the only one of the castles in Spain which is suitable for a home.

Then to Santo Tomas, and the collection of El Greco's paintings. We liked particularly the portraits of the Apostles. Robert liked the *Burial of the Count of Orgaz*—This is claimed to be the masterpiece. The work of the great Cretan grows more impressive with constant study—To the ordinary layman it may be difficult to admire at first view—But it is distinctive—there is much to admire as one studies the work more closely—and before one quite realizes it, he has come under the charm and greatness of the artist—and forever seeks another of the masterpieces of color and pattern.

A Spanish luncheon in the Spanish hotel and on to the cathedral. Here we saw more of El Greco's work. Here we saw a marvel in architecture and iron grill work about the choir—and a treasure house of art. This cathedral is indescribable— but it contains almost too much—There is more of an atmosphere of peace and heavenly contemplation in the more simple Gothic cathedrals like that of Segovia. One stops and marvels and wonders at the countless and priceless carvings, tapestries, bishops robes—paintings, windows, clocks and grill work—at the breathtaking altar—but one outside the Catholic religion feels no more religious than he would at a gigantic exhibit of art. One experiences the same reaction from both—that God

[10]*Rosselet Blake's parents and her sister Leontine were visiting.*
[11]*In 1942 my parents found just such a house to rent in La Jolla CA when the 10th Defense Battalion was training in San Diego in World War II*

is infinitely expressed in beauty and art—The infinite beauty in the Supreme Being is reflected in man's ideas which are made manifest in art. But more simplicity in design more singleness of purpose—seem to be better soil in which to sow a feeling for religion and for God. However it was a treat long to be remembered. The one regret is that the Cathedral is situated right in the midst of the town with houses and narrow streets encircling it—and there is no view of it to be had which does it justice. Notre Dame on the contrary can be seen from all sides—and stands out on one side of the Great Place most prominently. The interior of Toledo cathedral is said to be the finest of any in Europe.

We had tea in the Plaza de Zocodover and then visited the quaint little Posada del Sangre where Cervantes lived and wrote some of his immortal *Quijote*.

The ride home in the sunset was very beautiful.

July 14, 1931 – The Escorial

This was an expedition given by the Centro de Estudios Historicos where Robert and the other three Marine officers are enrolled in summer courses. We took our seats in buses early in the morning—another beautiful morning. And as the day progressed we grew warmer and warmer. A fine ride through the country into the rolling wooded country near the Escorial. A country like our California Monterey hills, rocky, wooded with pines and scraggly cedars—it brought a feeling of home.

Mr Martinez the leader spoke beautiful Spanish—so I was told—for I understand very little—but it sounded clear and bell-like. This great edifice—this monastery is grim and forbidding—Here there is no ornament at all; just a majestic pile of stone built with rows and rows of small windows and grey walls. There are some towers, in on one a stork has its nest. Thus began the pilgrimage through the miles and miles of corridor. The Library with its beautiful ceiling is a treasure spot—There are fine old manuscripts and fine paintings to be sure—a lovely inner garden—and an interesting room furnished by Philip the second—and the chapel and then the tombs of the Kings and royalty of Spain.

Later we visited the Palicito a small exquisite highly decorated little palace—tapestried walls—much carved ivories—Such a contrast to the great Escorial.

We had a most pleasant luncheon on the veranda of the attractive hotel—a lovely spot. The town is small—no particular business requires immediate attention. It has a good climate and is a summer resort for the city dwellers in Madrid during the hot weather. There is fine walking with many trails in the nearby hills.

A young Spanish professor from the University of Texas provided amusement with his droll remarks.

July 24, 1931 <u>Avila</u>

We joined the main Centro party at this quaint medieval town. The view from a distance is more impressive than the interior of this old city. It's the walls which give it its greatest distinction, though as the city of Santa Theresa it will forever remain one of the interesting cities of Spain. And it contains several churches which are of interest.

The drive to Avila was along a fine road and the ascent of the Guadarramas up a perfectly graded road with rocks on the mountains and fine views at intervals. After crossing the rather barren mountains we found heavy woods on the other side. The air was sweet and exhilarating.

The main plaza is unnotable—There are the usual narrow winding streets. We visited three churches—one built into the walls of the town—one very lovely in its simplicity and fine gothic archs and fine alter paintings. We took luncheon at the Hotel Inglais—then drove home by another route past a number of small adobe pueblos built on steep hillsides—barren and parched looking.

August 30, 1931. Navacerrada and La Granja & Madrid *(letter to Mrs. F. W. Wallace)*

How good it is to think of you at home. Your descriptions of England made us hope that we may include it in our wanderings. I hope to hear more of Papa's trip to Ireland.[12]

A few weeks ago we made an expedition to La Granja. It's an old palace in the foothills of the Guadarramas—a farm or grange where the royal family had a country home—There is nothing there but the palace and its beautiful gardens and fountains built on a hillside beneath a great blue mountain—and its outlying servants quarters and guard house—and a scattering of houses and a hotel. Many Madrileños have summer homes there too; it is a popular summer resort with a fine climate.

We took the train to the summit of the Guadarramas. Here we alighted at the end of the line and climbed a few feet higher to the pass—now we were about seven thousand feet high—And we began the descent of our ten mile trek to La Granja. We had Bobby with us. He ran about in circles chasing butterflies and lizards. For some time we remained on the fine paved highway but later followed a footpath through the woods—There were a variety of pine with a red bark something akin to the Sierra juniper. A very fine stand of them there were.

We had with us only three rolls and some chocolate a provision which was to prove to be very light.

We thoroughly enjoyed the walk through the woods. When we reached the end of the descent there was a quiet little stream meandering about. Here we waited for Bobby to wade and throw pebbles over the water. But the final two miles on the flat ground proved to be monotonous and tedious to Bobby. He rested frequently. But he continued on, needing a great deal of encouragement from the sidelines. After all, a child of ten with no previous practice can hardly be expected to do any better.

Having hiked ten miles we arrived in La Granja hot, dusty, dirty—disreputable I am sure. We had no luggage because of the walk— and most unfortunately had not written to engage a room. When we reached the only hotel in town we found that there were no rooms availble. Perhaps our trampy appearance caused the verdict. But it was a small hotel and at the height of the season and we later heard that reservations were made weeks in advance.

Spanish custom precludes an open dining room until nine or ten at night. It was only about half past four. We were hungry and tired. We did procure tea and rolls at the open air tables under the trees. We strolled in the exterior gardens. It was too late to see the palace and its famous gardens. At six o'clock we took the bus for Madrid. What a disappointment it was to be going back to the city when we had

[12]*Frederick Wallace was born in Londonderry. His family emigrated to California when he was an infant.*

planned to spend the week-end in the country. A little later we discovered that we could have stayed at a little pension if only someone had told us about it. The hotel clerk had said that there was no other hotel and we asked no further.

Still the sunset through the woods was very fine on our return journey.

We hope to go to La Granja again with Priscilla[13] who has just arrived. She spent several weeks in Paris and a week in Santander.

Friday night Robert's tennis club had a *verbena*—All players who participated in the tournament joined in giving the party. The majority of the members are Mexicans and Spaniards—But an English boy in our neighborhood invited Robert and Captain Kendall[14] to join. It proved to be a very jolly group of young people— and we danced on the tennis court. It is a tiring place for dancing but that did not spoil the fun.

Last night we went to the theatre and had driven downtown afterward— The theatre was a rather poor vaudevile. Our supper included *langosta*[15] and mayonaise—peach melba and coffee. It seemed to be a gay evening to us for our life here is quiet and studious.

One day not long ago I invited all the Spanish students' wives (the Marines) to tea at the Retiro. This is a beautiful Park in Madrid and there is an attractive cafe and tea place under the trees in a beautiful spot. Occasionally the other wives are the hostesses and we go to tea in one of the various places in Madrid—Here one sees all the Señoras and Señoritas taking their afternoon chocolate, dunking their bread or lady fingers in the thick syrupy mass which the Spaniards call chocolate. The Senoras wear *impertinentes*—lorgnettes and use them in accord with their name. They lift them and stare at every one who enters the tea place. It was really embarrassing at first. Alice Holmes[16] declares that she is going to wear her lorgnettes and stare also.

Sometimes at night, Robert and I take a walk down town winding about in all the little side streets we can find—watching the people—and looking into the windows that are open. The Spanish shop keeper usually draws down a heavy metal shutter over his shop window at night.

Sunday we drove out into the country to an old medieval castle—the picture of which appears in the *National Geographic* magazine for August. The article was written on Madrid. It contained many fine photographs and much interesting information. Near this castle is a lake—an artificial lake but beautiful nevertheless

---

[13]*Mrs. Thomas E. Watson. Her husband, then Major (later, Lt. General) Watson, USMC, was in Nicaragua.*

[14]*Don Kendall, later Lt. General USMC.*

[15]*Lobster.*

[16]*Wife of Captain (later Brig. General) Maurice Holmes.*

and much appreciated in this dry waterless country. You know that Madrid has a very light rainfall—Again, like California we have a long dry season.

Northern Spain on the contrary is very rainy—summer as well as winter. Here it is always sunny but dry and warm in the summer. Quite perfect it seems to me for it is never humid and enervating like Washington and the East Coast.

Tonight the Kendalls are giving a dinner party at the Hotel Nacional roof garden. The Marine colony is invited and will attend.

September 19, 1931 Toledo – Palomar – Peñalara *(letter to Mrs. F. W. Wallace)*

Yesterday we took Priscilla and the boys to Toledo. Robert had not visited there and I thoroughly enjoyed making another trip. It is a city which charms even more the second time than the first. We found our nice guide Julio Morales at Zocodover square. He came forward immediately and Spaniard that he is, appeared to remember me. We visited the same spots but saw others in addition—among them the charming hospital of Santa Cruz I regret that you missed it. It is a beautiful old building with a charming patio and some fine carved ceilings

At the end of our day we decided to walk to the station. It gives another vista of the town. There is a long flight of stairs at the towns edge with a glorious view of the river and valley below.

It was a privilege to see these interesting monuments and feast again upon the paintings—Robert was delighted with all that he saw. He even liked El Greco's paintings—to my surprise. He thought the cathedral very handsome—but he prefers the charm and beauty of the dwellings—He says that he prefers the places where people have lived to cathedrals.

Last Monday Mrs. Jimenez[17] took us for a drive. We went into the mountains and visited the club houses of the two Spanish walking clubs. They are within a few miles of each other near Navacerrada.

Peñalara is located nearer the summit and the end of the railroad. It is the club to which the King belonged. Mrs Jimenez has friends who are members and one very kindly is going to sponsor Robert. The Peñalara club house also is newer and very substantial in appearance for it is built of stone. Its sleeping quarters however were not so comfortable as those of the other club. The Spaniards seem to make up the majority of the Peñalara while the Alpine club consists of a majority of foreigners.

Upon our return we drove to an ancient Monestario—Palomar—Here all is antiquated beauty and quiet and peace.

We drove over the range to the Paris-Madrid road, and home.

Today Robert made his first expedition with Peñalara. They went to Escorial and from there walked fifteen miles. He enjoyed the Spaniards and the opportunity to speak Spanish in a social way. He says that they are excellent walkers. It was a thoroughly enjoyable outing. We find making Spanish contacts in a large city very difficult—Any sustained conversation in a social way is almost impossible for we have so few opportunities of meeting people The people in the Embassy cling to their American friends and the American colony does not mix—many of them have been here six years and longer and know not a word of Spanish. We have our teachers and the shop keepers and the servants with whom we may talk

---

[17] *Wife of Spanish poet Juan Ramón Jiménez, later Nobel Prize winner.*

but a little group of Spanish friends—no. It appears to be more practical to live in a smaller town. In that case it would be easier to become acquainted with some of the *gente*.

Tonight we are having dinner with Priscilla and her boys. She has secured a good maid which my Carmen sent her. Her apartment is by the side of ours. Priscilla and Alice and I take Spanish lessons at the Berlitz School. Our boys are in a class together.

October 24, 1931 Madrid

Yesterday and today it rained—the first real rain in five months. You no doubt have read of the change of Presidents here but it has made no decided rift. The same government is carrying on—only two vacancies had to be filled.

Recently there was a movement to put the Jesuits out of Spain—Some demonstrastions were held—nothing of a serious matter in Madrid. The Cortes is seriously considering the question. The Jesuits are the strongest and most influential sect politically and financially, but they have caused a great opposition because of their political ambitions and now may go at any time. Mrs Jimenez our friend brings us news of the Cortes for she is a daily visitor at the government meetings. She writes articles for her brothers' newspaper—a Spanish newspaper in New York—*La Prensa*

Recently Priscilla and I were guests of Mrs Jimenez at tea. She had another American lady, a Mrs deBoo who lived in Mexico three years—We had tea at the Lyceum—the women's club of Madrid. Mrs Jimenez was one of the leading figures who worked for the founding of the first women's club in Spain. Now that it is founded her interest has relaxed somewhat and she is busy with other things. She writes and runs a shop. Her husband is a poet. At the club we met and saw some of the other outstanding women. One was one of Spain's few women lawyers. She is on the committee drawing up the Constitution. She was a professor at the Centro this summer, teaching a course which I took.

Sunday morning we went to tea at the Women's Residencia. It is there that the women attending the university board. The girls in charge of it are friends of ours. We met many Spanish people at the tea and one who wished to exchange English lessons with Spanish. She is the sister of the Zubiarre brothers who are two of Spain's foremost modern painters. They paint Basque subjects.

Priscilla and I are still enjoying our Berlitz lessons. We like our teacher—She is very Spanish—and very refreshing.

Bobby is apparently enjoying the school which he attends in the afternoons. The instruction is in Spanish—arithmetic etc. He is reading *Don Quijote* in the literature class. The children play what they call *futbol* but it is really soccer. Bobby rides to and from school on his bicycle and wears a leather knapsack as the Spanish children do.

Since Robert went to Salamanca[18] Carmen has taken the best care of us. She is an excellent maid She takes all the responsibility. She even does the darning.

Tomorrow if it is not stormy Priscilla and the boys and I are going to Salamanca to see Robert. He is very much pleased with Salamanca and feels that he is progressing rapidly there. He is the only person speaking English in the town; he

---

[18]*After the end of the summer session at El Centro in Madrid, my father enrolled for the fall term at the historic University of Salamanca, 200 miles away.*

lives with a Spanish family—takes courses at the University and makes contacts with the students. In addition he has a private instructor. Salamanca was one of the three great Universities of the World during the Middle Ages—and its great man and educator Unamuno holds much interest.

A tea, and approaching wedding at the Embassy are the social events of note.

November 1, 1931 – Salamanca – first visit – Wedding

Priscilla has a movie camera with her. She has taken many pictures here but they require so much paraphernalia that it is often too much of a nuisance to be bothered.

I am planning a Thanksgiving dinner. We can buy turkeys and sweet potatos in Madrid.

Our trip to Salamanca was most interesting. It was a stormy week-end but we went regardless of weather. In a downpour of rain Robert and Don Antonio Boiza[19] took us through the University giving a lecture about its historical traditions. It is very picturesque The ceilings have fine carved and painted panels—And there is a very handsome carved wood balustrade on the principal stairway.

The hotel at Salamanca is modern—erected by the Patronato Nacional de Turismo—a tourist agency to attract people to Spain. We had two nice rooms and three meals a day for each of the three of us for only $5.50 for the <u>three</u>.

We met Robert's Spanish family—the one with whom he boards. It's a very old house with rooms on different levels and funny little doors in which one almost has to stoop in order to pass through. Robert's room is large and opens on a balcony overlooking a patio. It's attractive for summer but looks cold for the winter. The only means of heating is a brass *brasero*—a round brass container in which charcoal is burned. It is placed under a table with a long cloth and everyone sits at the table and places their feet upon the *brasero*.

Sunday the sun came out but it rained occasionally. Professor Boiza guided us again. We spent the morning in the old and new cathedrals—simple and very beautiful gothic cathedrals in sandstone. Boiza is a *Salamantino*. He loves his town and proves a most enthusiastic and sympathetic guide. Salamanca is still medieval—It gives the appearance of an old city but it has grown too. It may be the soft pinkish yellow color of the sandstone which gives it its charm—But to us it was Spain—the real Spain. Salamanca is full of parks and has many streets lined with trees. It looked very pretty. It also has a number of very handsome palaces and residences. The Palacio de Monterey belonging to the Duke of Alba is one of them—Also Unamuno's house and some churches and the University buildings and entrance.

[19]*Professor at the University of Salamanca; my father's tutor.*

Palacio de Monterey , Salamanca , 1930.

A river winds around the town and there are two fine bridges—one an old Roman bridge. The trees were still green— Altogether it seemed the prettiest and most liveable of all the old Spanish cities.

Monday was a clear day—but very cold. We walked again about the town. Then lunch—and then we took the train at two o'clock reaching home about six. I am delighted that Robert is progressing with his studies. He has no cares, responsibilities or interferences there. He is in a completely Spanish environment. Why come to Spain to learn Spanish if one hears only English among his companions?

Thursday the daughter of the commercial attaché was married to a secretary in the American Embassy. It was a pretty wedding. They were married in the little British church. Afterward the Ambassador and Mrs Laughlin gave a reception for them at the Embassy. Everyone was invited. There was dancing and music. The bride is a pretty young girl of only eighteen. Her father did not look any older than Robert. The groom was a man the father's age and a friend—Captain Holmes was our escort—the other husbands had classes and Robert is not here but Maurice took the ladies. He looked very handsome in his morning coat and gray striped trousers. We are going to drive with the Holmes this afternoon.

We study in the mornings—Bobby and I doing his lessons.[20] In the afternoon there is Spanish to study. Then we go for a walk, or go somewhere to tea, or perhaps to a movie. But the matineés here do not begin until seven o'clock. It's very cold at present.

---

[20]*Correspondence course from The Calvert School, Baltimore MD.*

November 8, 1931 Madrid *(letter to Mrs. F. W. Wallace)*

A delightful article in the *Cosmopolitan* by Montagne Glass entitled "Where Are those Old Spanish Customs" brought much amusement to Priscilla and me: Do read it if you can obtain one. I have also enjoyed Clara Laughlin's *So You are Going to Spain.*[21] She has combined appreciation of Spain and its lovely towns with history and art and much useful information about hotels, prices, roads and trains. We are planning a trip South in December; to cover Cordoba, Sevilla, Cádiz, Algeciras, Gibraltar, Ronda and Granada. With the help of Mrs Laughlin's book I have succeeded in planning an itinerary and a list of things to do in each place. It has been delightful fun.

Robert is coming home for Thanksgiving. It will be a month since we have seen him. We miss him a great deal. But he is contented with his progress and feels that this is the right thing to do.

---

[21] *Houghton, 1931.*

December 4, 1931 Thanksgiving in Madrid

We had a very pleasant Thanksgiving. We had a turkey dinner at two o'clock, inviting the Kendalls to join us. The Kendalls are giving up their apartment because Mrs Kendall is soon to go to England to visit her sister and parents. She left Madrid yesterday with the children. We had turkey and sweet potatoes and squash pie with whipped cream. No cranberries were to be had—canned or fresh.

In the evening we attended a Thanksgiving dinner dance given by members of the American Luncheon Club at a picturesque inn in the country not far from Madrid. It was very enjoyable.

Last Tuesday was a festive day—two teas were on the program—an informal tea by Mrs Gardiner whose husband is in General Motors here and Mrs Fletcher the wife of the military attaché gave a bridge tea. In Madrid one is served tea upon arrival at half past five and then bridge is on until eight or nine o clock because of the late dinner which is not served in Spanish households until ten or half past ten.

An American professor of Spanish at Southern California is one of our neighbors. He is on sabbatical leave. He is extremely interested—but said that he found more Spaniards to talk to in Los Angeles than in Madrid, at first.

We are very much occupied in preparations for our trip. As Robert is not here I am obliged to do it all. There is an application for a kilometric ticket to be made a week or so in advance. There are photographs to be taken for our *kilometrico*. We leave a week from Sunday. Robert will not arrive until a week from Sunday.

December 26, 1931 – *El Viaje al Sur -*
Cordoba *(letter to Mrs. F. W. Wallace)*

Your letter of the seventh of December arrived tonight. The post man came at eight o'clock at night for the first and only time today. It was good to reach home at four o'clock in the afternoon the day before Christmas.

We left Madrid Sunday the 13th of December arriving in Cordoba that night at six o'clock an eight hour journey. The country surrounding Cordoba is green There are pretty rolling hills. Andalusia is indeed much more pleasing country than Castile. After refreshing ourselves we had dinner and took a walk about the town in the dark. We were charmed. We saw men wearing the big brimmed flat crowned sombrero you see in pictures and always associate with Spaniards. There was an air of glamor cast over all.

The following morning in the sunlight we discovered that the town was not nearly so picturesque. We soon found the Mosque—I had done much reading about the mosque and hoped to be able to see it without a guide—But we were followed persistently by several who insisted that we should have a guide—We found the mosque very shabby on the exterior and somewhat marred by the baroque style church in the center of it. Nevertheless it is so enormous that even these deficiencies cannot really hurt it and we admired the intricate lacy Arabian workmanship and the multifarious types of columns—and lost ourselves in the forest of columns. We wandered about in it taking pictures for an hour or more. We admired the exquisite decoration of the *mihrabs*—places where the Koran was kept.

Later on we toured the town and the Mezquita bridge. A friend of our Madrid neighbors lives in the Alcázar. Gardino and her husband escorted us about the town, through the old Jewish quarter which is very picturesque. It was once the home of the wealthy but is a tenement district at present. Nonetheless the patios are still just as charming as when rich men inhabited them. We also visited a number of the homes of the present day wealth where we were allowed to see the ground floor.

Ruins of the palace of Abd-ar-Raman , Cordoba , 1931.

In the afternoon we drove out to to Abd-ar Rahman's ruined palace on the hills—a colossal place—but only foundation standing. It was razed when Ab-dar-Rahman III was defeated by some of his Moorish friends—We returned to Cordoba to have tea with the Scotts. I shall always remember their kindness.

Sevilla

We left that night for Sevilla where we arrived at half past nine. There we drove directly to the pension recommended by a friend which is the old palace of the Abades family on a circuitous street full of intriguing pations, in the old quarters. The pension appeared very picturesque. It was large and some very interesting looking Spanish people lived there. Again we were charmed and could hardly wait to put Bobby to bed so that we could explore Sevilla.

We suddenly found ourselves headed straight for the Giralda tower—an old moorish watch tower remaining from Arab days but now a part of the Cathedral. Next we discovered the romantic looking walls of the Alcázar. We strolled into the Court of Oranges with its orange trees and fountain. We strolled about in the moonlight and wished that we had gone to Sevilla to learn Spanish.

In the morning we saw the Cathedral. Again swarms of guides attacked us but we escaped and strolled slowly through the Patio of Oranges. Oh how cold it was! We entered the cathedral and I must say that nothing we have seen could compare to this. The morning light streaming in through the windows made it lighter than any other. It is a mammoth cathedral—the largest Gothic structure in the world, St Peters being the only one larger but it is not Gothic. The columns are so gigantic and tall that they seem to lose themselves in the heavens and man has a feeling of complete insignificance. We admired the windows too. Even the choir, which is placed in the center of the edifice as it is in all Spanish cathedrals, seems insignificant. One follows the arches down the nave as if there were no obstruction

In its size it gives a feeling of dignity and simplicity There are many interesting things stored here—paintings by Murillo, the very satisfying mural painting of the giant carrying the infant Jesus on his shoulders—the very fascinating tomb of Columbus—Then there was the Library of Columbus where 400 books owned by Columbus and his son are stored—rare old books on parchment exquisitely illuminated.

The Castle (or Alcázar), a remnant of the Moorish kings but made into the present form by Pedro the Cruel, is a story book castle. The entrance gate and wall is battlemented. The coat of arms of the Kings of castile, the Lion and the Castle is painted on the gates. The gardens surrounding it are most beautiful. Here we spent an hour or more walking about. Later we went through the Castle. It was used by the kings as a residence until Alfonso XIII—Hence it is only since the republic that visitors have been allowed to go to the second story. The King's bedroom was very plain—both in furniture and hangings. The Queen's room was more elaborate. It contained a very ornate bed which was used by Isabella II. We saw the *Infantas* rooms—and all the royal quarters.

Gardens of Peter the Cruel's palace , Sevilla , 1931.

The center of the Palace is the original Moorish portion. The mosaic work is exquisitely delicate; they say it is as fine as the Alhambra and built at approximately the same time.

The following day we took a guide to take us to Italica—the remains of an old Roman town recently excavated. Many of the vases and statues found here are placed in museums in Sevilla. It is across the river from Sevilla about six miles away. Upon crossing the river we first went through Triana, the gypsy town, and also the home of one of the most famous ceramic factories in Spain. They make lovely pottery by hand. It was interesting to see the clay being spun about on a wheel until it was just the right shape and then put aside to dry. Later it was decorated and glazed.

Next we went on to a deserted monastery where Guzman el Bueno is buried and then on to Italica There are the ruins of a Roman amphitheatre—All that remains are the ridges in the ground and the aisles and arches around the outside. There are the remains of paved roads and almost perfect tile mosaic floors—the colors fresh, the tiles unbroken. These excavations took place within the last four years and are consequently only the beginning.

In the afternoon we returned to Seville and our guide took us through the picturesque Santa Cruz quarter, adjoining the Alcázar. Here many artists and famous people have lived. It once was the home of the aristocrats. Washington Irving lived here for a time. Not far away from the castle is the house of the Barber of Seville made famous by the opera.

We were taken to see three of the most beautiful houses of Seville, the home of the Duke of Alba and two others. We like the Alba house very much—we of course only saw the patio and the first floor apartments. But the house we saw later—the home of another Duke was handsome and more impressive. There were choice chests and objects of art everywhere. I really think that the Spaniards are most amiable to allow people to go even on the first floor of their homes. Of course one pays—No doubt they are not averse to taking in a little cash. The doorman and butler who showed us through were quite the best looking *servidumbre* I have ever seen. The inner patio was exquisite—Even on a hot summer day one could not fail to feel cool and refreshed in such a place with the trickle of falling water constantly splashing.

Next we climbed the Giralda tower. Instead of stairs there is an inclined runway. It makes the ascent very easy. From the top we had a beautiful sunset view of the city.

The charm of our pension waned the second day. The food was poor—and so was the plumbing. As for heat, all we had was a copper brazier under a table. One had to sit at the table to keep warm placing his feet on the brazier where a small charcoal fire was burning. Another time I should waive the call of the picturesque and go to the Hotel Inglaterra The following day Robert and Bobby took photographs. We all went for a walk in the afternoon. We see our cities thoroughly for we do most of our sightseeing walking. One afternoon we drove around the city and the Exposition grounds.

Cádiz

Friday morning we took a train to Cádiz. It was good to smell salt air. We arrived there at two oclock. The Hotel Atlantico on the ocean quite charmed us. We had two rooms and two baths overlooking the ocean. It is off season; we were given good rates. three dollars a day a person for the rooms, baths and three meals. Excellent food and service, and the choice rooms of the hotel. It seemed like a palace after the pension experience. We were unable to look up Papa's friend Mr

Ajuca, for we had only a few hours and Robert wanted to walk about getting photographs.

The following morning we took the early bus to Algeciras. It proved to be a glorious drive around the Bay of Cádiz and across beautiful country to the ocean again where we could see Trafalgar Bay and Africa across the Straits. It was clear and sunny in Cádiz but we could see a storm brewing and black clouds near the ocean. Just before we reached Algeciras it began to rain and was very disagreeable there. We had planned to take a private car and drive to Gibraltar spending four hours there. But the rain made such an expedition unattractive hence we took the 12 o clock train for Ronda. The mists obscured a clear view of the famous rock but we did see its great grey bulk looming up in the rain. It seemed even larger and more impressive than I had imagined. We had nothing but a sandwich and some oranges to eat. The poky little train carried no dining car. We were almost four hours going eighty miles.

Ronda

Foolishly we had made no reservations and almost failed to be taken in by Mrs Law at the very attractive English hotel on the bluff. She was having work done—painting and central heating installed. But we must have looked forlorn for she did take us in after saying that she had no rooms. She gave us two small single rooms and put an extra cot in one. We were delighted It was a feeling of great relief and calm that we sat down to tea between two beautiful wood fires in the living room. A family of English people from Gibraltar with a little boy about Bobby's age attracted us. Bobby had a game of dominoes with the English boy. A Spanish family also had a boy about Bobby's age. There were about eight other guests. We wandered in the gardens on the edge of the cliff. Ronda is built on a high plateau at the top of a cliff, overlooking a valley and winding river. At one place across the chasm there are three bridges, the modern bridge is highest, and there are two others of Moorish and Roman days. It is probably the most picturesque of all the Spanish towns we have seen. We spent two days here enjoying the town, the Moorish king's palace, the lovely old homes and the breath-taking views. We were followed about on one of our photographing expeditions by a crowd of children saying "moneys" "moneys" "moneys." The English have taken a great fancy to Ronda and the beggars have learned English from them. The mountains surround it and it is a strategic center for interesting hikes. It is said to be the stronghold for smugglers of the background for "Carmen."

Granada

We left Monday for Granada reaching there after a seven hour ride—the train crawls along. Here we found ourselves located in another most attractive place— an English pension reccomended by friends. It was on top of a hill above the Alhambra—which was close by. We had a gorgeous view of the town and the Sierra. It was farm house style—very artistic by simple—almost crude. We had fireplaces in each room and enormous ones downstairs. Nice people—Excellent food—delicious afternoon teas. Again we made our first exploration at night and by moonlight. Ever since reading *The Alhambra* in High School I had dreamed of seeing the Alhambra by moonlight. I had planned the trip so that we should have moonlight when here. With visions of "Moonlight in the Court of Lions" we hurried down to the old Moorish palace only to find it closed. After much banging on the gate we aroused a guard who told us that we could not enter unless we made arrangements for it beforhand and paid a large fee $7.00 or so. It would be reasonable for a party but for a mere couple seemed a bit steep. They say that the cost is for the extra guards needed to keep the place open at night.

The great trees and wooded avenues surrounding the Alhambra were beautiful. There is also a fine guard tower which is very picturesque. It was extremely cold the following day when we went again to the palace. The water in the pools was frozen. The fountains were not playing. In such cold atmosphere it hardly seemed possible that people had ever lived in such an open airy palace. But the colors were exquisite, the workmanship superb. It was all and more, than I had expected. We met a cultured and charming Spanish gentleman Señor Flores. He is the chief guide—but appeared to be rather a student or scholar. We had completed a tour of the place when we encountered him—yet he showed us many things we had not seen—the room where Washington Irving lived while he wrote the tales—a balcony where harem ladies peeped through tapestries into the Court of Nuzettes. The ladies were never allowed in the court on state occasions but could see all that went on from their balcony. Señor Flores also pointed out an exquisite vista with the snow capped Sierra in a straight line with the murmuring splashing fountain in one of the tiny gardens. We visited the old citadel later. Robert who had been a bit disappointed went away feeling that the Alhambra was indeed a charming place.

Patio of the Alhambra , Granada , 1931.

After luncheon we visited the Cathedral to see the tombs of Ferdinand and Isabella, exquisite sculptures in stone. Later we drove about the town and ended up at the Gypsy Caves where we saw an excellent exhibition of a gypsy dance the "Flamenco". But paid dearly for it—not having made a bargain with them before being lured into the cave. Always make your bargains with Spanish people in advance.

The following cold, grey and forbidding day we saw the Generalife—the summer palace with its fountains and exquisite gardens. The hot tea and food at the pension were most appealing. There was snow in the mountains that night. Some English girls and the Spanish waitresses at the pension were making some Christmas decorations after supper and sang English and Spanish Christmas carols.

We were glad to come home to Madrid Wednesday night. We took a *coche—cama.* We were delayed several hours by a freight train off the track, hence it was dark: and Christmas Eve when we reached home.

A friend had ordered a tree and I had bought some ornaments before leaving—so it was not long until we had the tree decorated. Carmen welcomed us heartily. It is good to come to such a welcome.

Christmas day we had a friend—a Scotchman name Ewing—take dinner with us. Later, in the afternoon we all went over to the Holmes to spend a pleasant *rato.*

Christmas Eve here is almost like Halloween at home—it is so noisy. Every one goes out into the streets and they beat drums and tambourines and sing carols in a minor key. Earlier, about ten thirty the families gather and have a supper of fish. The people in the streets wear gay costumes and they remain there until midnight Then they go to mass. We heard the sad plaintive singing and beating of drums almost like tom-toms on our street, Velázquez. Then the noisy clamor of the bells of the church across the street burst upon us at midnight. It was a strange Christmas Eve.

Calle de Velázquez in the snow, Madrid , Christmas 1931.

(letter to Mrs. F. W. Wallace)   **December 29, 1931**

Here are some photographs of our trip South. When I look at them, they seem a great many—but when I think of all the mental pictures I have of each place we visited, they seem extremely inadequate.

Traveling in Spain, one speaks little Spanish. In all the hotels English is spoken by some-one at least. Our appearance is against us. We look American or English and they promptly begin in our language though we may painstakingly start a question in our best Spanish.

Robert returned to Salamanca yesterday. He says it is like going to the front in war-time. There are only a few more months to be gotten through with alone. I am planning to go to Salamanca in April to spend our last two months there.

February 12, 1932

Robert has been with us six days—Carnival week. There were masked balls, people on the streets in costume, parades of people inh carriages and cars, impressive floats with prizes for the best costume and vehicle. Neither the parades nor the costumes were particularly beautiful. It was the *gente*, the poorer people who took part—but they were gay and happy. It was the spirit of festivity which gave the parade its charm. What a pity that the people do not wear their charming regional costumes.

We attended one of the masked balls. It was given by the Cartoonists Society and was held in one of the theatres. There were a few interesting costumes but the majority were not striking. We did not dress but wore Spanish combs in our hair. I have a pretty blue one, but it is so large that it is difficult to wear with my short hair.

One night when Robert was here we visited the oldest restaurant in Madrid—the Antigua Casa de la Botín. It was there that famous writers like Lope de Vega and other kindred spirits used to gather. It is small and old fashioned—The place is famous for its suckling pig; a dish a little too rich for me.

One of Robert's professors visited in Madrid at Christmas time. His parents live here. His father is an Army officer. Don Manuel[22] had luncheon with us. I was surprised and pleased to see the ease with which Robert carried on a converstion. Don Manuel stayed all afternoon. I was able to understand much of the conversation but said little—for a good reason.

We spend much time in book shops. Robert is buying many books; mostly history and literature We have three editions of *Don Quijote*.

We went to call on some friends last night. Robert is having a suit made—a pretty light mixture—brown predominantly but with some lavendar. The suits are made of English tweeds by a military tailor; the whole, material and labor costs only three hundred pesetas or about thirty dollars at the present rate of exchange. To a Spaniard it is sixty dollars and they consider the tailor expensive.

We continue to have glorious weather. But today it is raining.

<u>Sunday morning</u>

This morning we awakened to find snow on the roofs and gardens across the street. It is very pretty but does not appear to be enduring.

This afternoon Mrs Jiménez is giving a tea at her shop to which I am going.

February 17, 1932

Two weeks ago I went up to Salamanca for the week-end. Robert had found a pretty regional costume and wanted me to see it. The Salamanca *charra* costume is said to be the prettiest of all regional costumes. It is very elaborate and very expensive. The finest ones are beyond our means—but the one we bought is very pretty—gold spangles embroidered on black wool skirt and gold spangles and colored stones on the apron with purple silk ruffle. The skirt has a broad band of purple velvet on it—The bodice is black satin covered by a purple velvet surplice embroidered in gold and white net veil and scarf embroidered in gold spangles—String upon string of gold beads around the neck and gold pins in the hair make it very attractive. There's a special headdress also, hair parted in the center and drawn into two round buns over each ear, surrounded by gold pins. The skirt has three petticoats.

The ride to Salamanca was delightful for it was snowing—it was the third day of snow in the mountains—all was a beautifil white—quiet and peaceful. I left here at half past three and arrived in Salamanca at half past eight—And it

---

[22]*Manuel Cardenal. He became a lifetime friend.*

was bitterly cold there. Sunday was a feast day and many country people came to church in regional costume. I saw a number similar to mine. It was a pretty sight. Some wore brightly colored woolen skirts embroidered in black wool with colored handkerchiefs on their heads. I have some of the woolen handkerchiefs—they would make attractive scarfs.

The Ambassador amd Mrs Laughlin gave a very delightful musical recently for the President and Mrs Zamora of Spain. We were the only Americans invited outside the Embassy itself. The music was delightful—Segovia is a well known guitarist, one of Spain's foremost—and Cubiles at the piano. Cubiles plays in the Madrid Symphony. We enjoyed it very much. At one o'clock a delicious supper was served.

On Washington's birthday the Laughlins gave a very pleasant tea.

Yesterday I attended a delightful concert with two men singers as the stars. Mrs Jiménez went with me. The singers sang whole selections from operas but I particularly enjoyed the Spanish songs which they did especially well.

Today we are going to a Philharmonic Symphony at six 'clock—Concerts are frequent and very reasonable in Madrid—the best seats cost six pesetas, or less than sixty cents

Robert has made some interesting friends. They meet every evening at the café for an hour or two of conversation They call the gathering a *tertulia*. A glass of beer or coffee is the most popular order—This group is the young married men of Salamanca—business men—but one wonders where they work. Here Robert improves his Spanish and picks up the current phrases.

When Spanish people ride in trains or buses for several hours they take along a lunch which they pass to anyone in their compartment. It is a friendly gesture. Mrs Jiménez said that one should accept a little. They always shake hands with all other travellers upon leaving the train at their destination and wish the others *un buen viaje*.

Last Sunday Bobby and I went to the Rastro. I bought two paisleys and some linens and a charming copper water jug and a black lace *mantilla*. I am collecting some things to take home. If there is anything that you would like please let me know.

(letter to Mrs. F. W. Wallace)   **February 5, 1932**

Tito Ruffo was here recently and was to have sung. I invited senorita Alcaide to have dinner with me and go to hear him. We had dinner together but the concert was post-poned on account of his illness. I remember hearing him once in Berkeley.

There is an excellent series of Symphony concerts being given every Sunday morning.

Last Saturday was a pleasant day. I called upon a friend who lived with us in our first pension. It was the first time that I had rung the bell at that pension since leaving seven months ago. But the maid who opened the door greeted me like a life long friend. One might have thought that we had lived there years instead of a month. Spanish servants are most effusive and are more like friends than a menial. I had expected to tell them who I was. But the maid cried *"Señorita commo está?"* And all sent *"muchos recuerdos"* to the señorito. Miss Reed entertained me by a recital of her trip to Munich. She is a musician.

Mrs Jiménez invited me to tea at her house with several Spanish ladies. It proved to be very delightful. They all speak far better English than I do Spanish—and for a time they spoke English through courtesy but fortunately they became interested in some affairs of the Women's Club and lapsed into Spanish the greater part of the time. Mrs Jiménez is charming as you know and her friends are quite as interesting as she is. Her husband is a poet and she is a writer.

Recently a friend and I saw Carmen Diaz in "Solero." The two authors were present—bowing and smiling. Going to a Spanish play is still a sort of game to me. I listen eagerly and am delighted when I understand a phrase, and rejoice when I can understand a whole sentence. It is much more delightful than understanding a teacher.

We have had glorious weather only one week of cold weather in November and perfectly lovely sunshiney days almost continually. Madrid is indeed a place of sunshine. At present it is warm and springlike.

Recently I gave an informal tea for eight.

Last Tuesday some friends and I visited the Royal Palace. The dinginess of the exterior is forgotten when one begins to ascend the magnificent staircase—There are exquisite tapestries—handsome official banquet and reception halls—No doubt it was even finer when the Kings lived there. It is very spacious and handsomely furnished. There seems to be no end of official reception rooms. The throne room in comparison is small—one of the smallest. It has some exquisite bronze statues in it and is furnished in red. The red velvet on the walls looked a bit worn, but it may have been the way the light struck it. We saw only the official rooms. The private quarters are being renovated and are not open to the public at present.

One of the attendants had been with the King over thirty years. He told us about the last day that the King was in the Palace. He said that after the King left there were no guards nor soldiers to guard the Palace. The crowds were shouting

"*Viva la republica*" in the streets. The Queen and Infantas were wondering what they would do—what would happen. But it was a peaceful leavetaking. We saw King Alfonso's desk with a calendar turned to the day of departure. Just as he left it. Beside the dining room which is large there is a banquet room with a table seating eighty people, which can be made to accomodate one hundred and twenty five. There is a magnificent view from some of the windows overlooking the West Park and gardens.

Sunday Bobby and I walked out the Castellana in the sunshine to the Natural History Museum. Later we went to the Prado—exploring the rooms downstairs. Miles of pictures and sculptures. Many pictures are hung in a very bad light—We found some very interesting Flemish paintings.

March 5, 1932

Bobby and I went to Salamanca to meet Robert and from there took the four o'clock bus to Zamora. It was not as interesting as some other tours. The country was the scene of much fighting in early days and is barer than usual. The cathedral and one or two palaces are the chief points of interest.

The Plaza Mayor is small and not very interesting Our hotel was comfortable and served satisfactory meals. Hotel Suiza. Spent the night and took the Sunday afternoon train to Salamanca.

March 29, 1932

The prices of food at home astonished me. Living is about three times as expensive here. The maids buy in small quantities of course as there are no frigidaire nor even refrigerators nor any decent pantries. The poor people live on *garbanzos* which are cheap, but butter and eggs and vegetables are expensive. At home even before food prices went down we could manage our food bills from forty to sixty dollars a month. but here where Robert is with us they are 850 pesetas a month or about seventy five dollars which to a Spaniard is $150. Which is outrageous! We do no entertaining and do not have variety nor the great abundance of food in the house that we do at home.

We spent a happy week in Salamanca with Robert. We lived in a *pension* on the Plaza Mayor. The food was excellent—the room fair—but very cold. Salamanca is colder than Madrid. We took our books along and Bobby had his lessons.

View of the Plaza Mayor from the balcony of the Blakes' pension, Salamanca , 1932.

Robert studies all morning; has two classes in the afternoon—goes to his *tertulia* in the cafe from seven to nine and then comes home for dinner. After dinner he studies again.

One day he and Bobby and a high school class went up to Los Saltos del Duero where a dam is being constructed. One afternoon Bobby and I walked out into the country It was a glorious sunny day. There is a barracks on the edge of town and as we walked we saw the soldiers drilling on a large field. A soldier blew a bugle. It is good to hear a bugle again. It reminds me of Quantico and Mare Island.

We walked ten kilometers—to a little village near a group of trees—five kilometers from Salamanca. The road which we took was a popular one for *paseos*. A Spanish *paseo* is a leisurely saunter a short distance out from Salamanca, and much talk and resting. One seldom sees a biker as we do at home.

Communion Thursday is the only day when the women wear mantillas in modern days. So they come in swarms in black, with black mantillas and high combs. The communion is in celebration of the Last Supper. After communion at twelve o'clock the women walk around the Plaza in groups. Even the plainest señorita looks lovely. The lines of the Spanish people and large comb make a lovely picture—For a few hours it was Spain of the story books and pictures. But after luncheon the girls appear in brightly colored coats and little berets tilted on one side and to the back of their heads—and again it is modern Spain.

We attended the communion service of the university faculty, held in the University chapel. The professors wore their black gowns and all carried tall taper candles. Each professor took communion and knelt with his tall lighted candle. It was a pretty sight—The mass was well executed. After mass the professors slowly marched out after the priests, still holding their candles and paraded around the University plaza singing. They were followed by a crowd.

One evening we were invited to Don Manuel's house He teaches Latin in the high school. He is young, a few years younger than Robert. Both he and his wife attended the University of Madrid. The señora is a student, doing some research work on a book on grammar for Menendez Pidal, who is head of the Royal Academy and a leader in educational movements. Their home was interesting—old with low ceilings—old chests and interesting linens.

We were served chocolate in true Spanish style—thick and syrupy. One does not drink it—one "dunks"—either a piece of bread or cake is dipped into the chocolate and eaten. *Churros* are sometimes served with chocolate. They have the color and appearance of a doughnut but are much lighter, thinner and crisper and come in very large circles. When we first arrived in Madrid we used to enjoy taking tea downtown in order to watch the señoras "dunking" their chocolate. It is quite correct and everyone apparently does it. There is no other way to take chocolate. With the chocolate, which is sweet, is served a large piece of spun sugar which looks like a long white meringue. A glass of water or a glass of milk is used to dissolve the sugar. Then this beverage is sipped alternately with "dunking" the chocolate. In addition very sweet pastries are served. It is something of an ordeal for me not accustomed to it but the Spaniards are kind and friendly—and one tries to enter into new customs.

We called upon the Boizas and had chocolate with them. But as it was Good Friday we had a simple repast of chocolate, *churros* and bread. In this family there are seven children and most delightful and cultured parents—Don Antonio is a university professor, brilliant and charming. I admired an old tile, not thinking of the Spanish custom of offering whatever is admired. He told me that it was mine since it had pleased me. But of course I did not take it. One is not supposed to accept. Instead one should say—"May you enjoy it many years," or something to that effect. Don Antonio put the tile back on the library shelf.

Sunday we had a young Spanish friend of Robert's in to dinner. He was preparing to take an examination for a government position. He is an interesting conversationalist and talked as we walked about the plaza—about languages and Spanish customs.

In Spain women seldom go to a hospital—they have their babies at home—they do not weigh them when they are born nor do they watch their weight afterward. No one seems to have scales. I discovered all this through a visit to a young mother. They give very young children coffee. They keep their children up late—the poorer people walking with them in the streets until one 'o clock in the morning—and many of the more afluent classes take their babies to the theatre night—bringing a nurse along to care for them. How much more comfortable for all concerned if nurse and child had stayed at home!

It was difficult to leave Salamanca. But we are expecting orders at any time now.

Ready made clothes are not satisfactory here as they are at home. One has them made to order. Even this is not always a success. I had a dress made last fall which does not fit properly. It takes much time and thought to go about visiting "openings" showing latest Paris fashions—and after that is done—one has all the fittings to go through with. My Spanish teacher and I went to see some new models at a modistas who used to sew for the Infantas. Senorita Alcaide had a very attractive gown made there. I found a model I liked and am having one made. Senorita Alcaide is very vivacious friendly and likeable. Her father was an army official killed in the Spanish American war. Her mother and sister passed away recently. She is living alone in an adorable little apartment with painted furniture which she painted herself—a bright red with blue shelves—and Basque linen curtains at the windows with red and blue stripes. She has much Talavera pottery which is very decorative. She offered me some *mazapan* a sweet from Toledo—which I enjoyed very much.

April 23, 1932

Ciudad Rodrigo

We made this delightful trip with the Griffiths—a professor of Spanish from University of Southern California and his wife. Robert met us in Salamanca and we all had luncheon together at the Viuda de Fraile, taking a four o'clock bus for Ciudad Rodrigo. A classmate of Robert's at the university of Salamanca made the trip too for it was his home pueblo. It was a long ride through rolling country with trees resembling our live oaks in California.

We arrived about seven o'clock walking around the town in the twilight. The Patronato hotel is located in an old Castle, that of Henry II The dining room looks out over the river and plain. It was a quiet tranquil sky. Sunday morning Robert and I took a walk entirely around the town on the top of the city walls. There is a moat and a drawbridge—all in good condition. We climbed the castle tower. The *cura* there arrived to show us the town. It is a clean little town off the trail of tourists—There are no beggars nor guides visible. There are some delightful old houses. As we walked about taking pictures Robert found it difficult to get a good view of the cathedral. A lady in a balcony called down to ask if we would like to go up there to take the photograph. Of course she knew the *cura* or she would not have invited us in—Still it was a kind friendly thing to do. We enjoyed seeing her house with its fine tiled fireplace int the kitchen.

Gate to Henry II tower, Ciudad Rodrigo, 1932.

We felt pretty medieval in our castle. The place is a delightful one for a rest—excellent food—a picturesque lodging with some lovely hand made and embroidered tapestries on the walls—an air of quiet and peace—and no tourists. If only we could stay another year in Spain we should return here for a longer stay. I saw a string of the prettiest gold beads I have ever seen, here.

Monday morning early we left for Salamanca. Robert returned to Madrid with me to pack for we decided to stay with Robert in Salamanca until we go home.

May 8, 1932

La Alberca and Las Batuecas

We rented a car and took Andrés, Don Manuel's son, with us. He is about Bobby's age. It was lovely in the springlike country. This part of Spain is cold and spring is late. We passed many orchards in bloom, those in the mountains near La Alberca were particularly lovely. The mountains are about the height of the Santa Cruz mountains in California. This mountain village was the most picturesque we had seen. The houses are taller with peaked roofs and much woodwork on the upper part like Normandy houses—The streets are narrower and cobbled. Every nook and corner of La Alberca would make an exquisite picture.

Blake family with Andrés Cardenal , La Alberca , 1932.

Around the edge of town is a stream, orchards in bloom and rambling stone walls A sweet little girl in a long skirt and kerchief was our guide. She took nothing but some of the children in their quaint clothes posed for a picture for Robert and he gave them a peseta to spend for candy "*para todos*"—They all skipped away saying *"Para todos, Para todos"*. Here all the people wear their regional costumes.

We found a congenial group of women with whom we chatted for some time—and even took their picture when a man strolled up and we insisted upon taking him too. He entered willingly into the plan and posed very handsomely for us.

From La Alberca we drove over the summit of the mountains, down into a small enchanting valley where Las Batuecas is located. It is an old foresaken monastery. But there is still an inn there. From the summit down into the valley was fourteen kilometers of hairpin curves. The road follows the old foot trail used by the monks. There was no road at all then. The monastery is in ruins surrounded by orchards and vines. The beautiful Judas tree or "red bud" was in bloom. Nearly all monasteries are located in beautiful surroundings. There were little rock shelters located high up on the hillsides where the monks lived in solitude and in prayer.

The man in charge of the inn was a student priest but he never completed his studies. A young girl conducted us to various view points and shrines.

We had a good meal and enjoyed sitting by the stream where Bobby and Andrés played for several hours.

On our return through La Alberca some of the townspeople mistook our car for the governor's car (he was visiting the neighborhood). We were cheered lustily.

Near Salamanca we witnessed a round-up of *toros*. They were driven from the fields by whooping cowboys—into a small walled courtyard and from there prodded into another smaller one and from there herded and prodded into wooden cars which in turn rolled to a station and attached to trains to be sent to bull rings all over Spain.

May 17, 1932

<u>Valladolid, Simancas, Alaejos, Tordesillas</u>

We were all three guests of Don Antonio and joined the excursion of his class in bibliography. There were nineteen of us—The students sang popular Spanish songs in the bus. Everyone was very jolly and friendly. The country was very green. Stops at various small castilian pueblos gave us an idea of typical pueblo life. There is little of much architectural merit but an occasional cathedral or woodcarving in some small church. There was one such that was exquisite—some very fine carving in the dome.

Valladolid appears to be almost entirely modern—not old as Salamanca appears. The University library was fascinating with its treasure of old books, a thousand years old; illuminated in color. A few old houses are all that is to be seen of historical interest. We had a jolly luncheon in a restaurant.

On the ride home we stopped twice, once at Simancas where the archives of Spain are kept in an old castle. And we stopped at Tordesillas where we saw more exquisite wood carvings in the cathedral. The children of the town followed us about. They did not know what to make of us—As some of the university girls had put some sprays of white blossoms in their hats—at first the children asked if we were having a wedding.

June 4, 1932

Burgos

We left Salamanca alone, Bobby and I, after much talking to railroad ticket men trying to make them give me a receipt for my tickets. We need receipts in order to get our money back from the government, but it is not customary nor allowable for Spanish railroad ticket men to give receipts. Hence I had to be satisfied with the ticket with the ticket sellers signature and the date stamped upon it. Robert met us at Medina del Campo.

In Burgos we stopped at the Hotel Avila. We arrived at four and immediately explored walking to the top of one of the hills overlooking Burgos and its airy cathedral. Here on this hill was the ruin of the Cid's old home. In this castle the Cid was married. We had a fine view of the town and country. Now it is a vivid green. The cathedral dominates all. The exterior is very pleasing. I was captivated. There are only a few relics in Burgos of ancient days—but one of the finest is the old main gate. It is very medieval—The *Casa de Cordon* which belonged to a noble family is fascinating. Here Columbus was received by Ferdinand and Isabella after his second voyage. There is a particularly beautiful patio.

As for the cathedral, I was entranced by it. I gloried in the many degrees of light and shade in it. It is influenced by the Cologne cathedral for its bishop made a trip to Germany and became won over to that style. It is more feathery and inspiring than many Spanish cathedrals. It appeared too ornate in places. Sevilla cathedral is the most impressive but this one is beautiful in its lights and shades and its lacy exterior. We first saw it in the evening and that is an ideal time to get the feeling of a cathedral.

We wandered along the river which is very pretty. There is a park along its banks which adds to the attractiveness of the city.

We spent the following morning seeing the cathedral in detail—and the afternoon in seeing Las Cartijas a beautiful monastery. We left at half past five for Pamplona.

June 6, 1932

Pamplona

A charming Basque town where the French were defeated several times when they grew too ambitious and desired to cross the Spanish boundaries. It is located high on a bank above the river surrounded by mountain peaks. Very little remains to give evidence of its historical past other than the high walls, the three moats, the fortifications and citadel—which all testify to its having been a frontier town.

The cathedral is interesting from the rear. It has a charming patio and attractive cloisters. But what a dreary facade! An uninteresting modern imitation of Greek Roman style—It might be a bank or a railroad station.

The most attractive thing about Pamplona is its situation. We stopped at Hotel La Perla which is also Gran Hotel—

June 7, 1932

San Sebastian

The bus trip from Pamplona is only two and a half hours through exquisite Basque country. I shall never forget the great gray stone portals through which we passed in leaving the valley near Pamplona. There we climbed a steep canyon overlooking a green river. The mountains grew more and more rugged, with granite summits. The valleys were fertile and green and cultivated to the hilltops in different shades of green and yellow. The wild flowers were in bloom everywhere mostly mustard and dandelions also red poppies and some blue flowers.

The Basque houses are very picturesque built of stone of a soft yellow hue—with woodwork—and built on the lines of a Swiss chalet, but they have red tiled roofs. After passing through Tolosa we reached San Sebastian.

Here we stopped at Hotel Arana, another small hotel but the service was excellent. We spent the first morning walking around the concha beach and later the boys had a swim. We walked around the Monte Urgula on the beautiful wide driveway. It is a mountain peninsula. It makes a popular walk for many people were out that evening. A glorious sunset and the lights began to twinkle.

Wednesday morning we walked to the top of Monte Urgula where there are ruins of an old castle, also a beautiful natural park.

In the afternoon we hired a car and drove through the greenest most fertile country we had seen in Spain Also along a rocky sea coast. In one place we came upon a bay with a rocky island called The Rat for it does look like an enormous rat from a distance. Here there is a monument to Elcano, the first man to go around the world and to return to Spain. Magellan died in the Philippines. Elcano was with his expedition and his ship alone returned. We saw a castle of the Duke of Granada.

In Zumaya we visited the home of Zoluaga the painter. He has a delightful studio containing many of his most interesting paintings. I like his portraits of Basque and Spanish types best of all. The museum is on his own property which is a peninsula jutting out into the sea. He has a charming house and grounds. His daughter and her husband and some friends were there playing *pelota*. We stopped for a moment to watch the famous Basque game.

We drove on to Loyola where Saint Ignatius founder of the order of Jesuits was born and visited the house and monastery. It is a beautiful location—

But the real jewel of the trip was the drive from Loyola by a winding road which climbed the mountains some 2,000 feet to a charming village, hanging to the mountainside, Regil. At the summit we stopped and got out of the car sitting by the roadside where we gloried in the view—mountains ranging away far below and beyond—the valley itself far below The fields of different shades of green appeared to be velvet—and the soft brown ploughed ground appeared velvety in its texture from that height. The green reached up and up to the very granite summit of the mountain on our right The farm houses of soft cream with their red tiled roofs were set off by the green fields. It is said to equal in loveliness the country in the lower Alps in Switzerland. These high fields at our feet were full of blue columbine. Our chauffeur was a cultured well read man who loved the beautiful country and enthusiastically pointed out every charm of the view while he discussed Spanish literature. He recommended many books to Robert to read. We were loathe to leave that charming spot.

The return drive was delightful and the final pearl was the exquisite view of blue bay San Sebastian with its white Concha beach below, with the green velvety country and mountains in the background, from Monte Iguelda. Around on the ocean side was a sunset ocean view similar to many in California—the setting sun made a golden path over the waters. But we turned back again to drink in the beauty of the San Sebastian bay. I shall always remember it.

June 8th 1932

Paris, France

We left San Sebastian in the evening at sunset. We had a beautiful ride to Irun along the bay. It was a beautiful Spain we left just at dark. At Hendaye we changed trains to cars with the most luxurious sleepers I have seen. Even nicer than the Sud Express. There was only one berth in each compartment—and two compartments adjoined, making a most spacious effect. We rode through beautiful green country as we were nearing Paris. In Paris it was warm summer weather. We went to the Belfast Hotel just off the Arc de Triomphe on Avenue Carnot.

Bobby and I took a walk to the home of the American Ambassador and the Trocadero and the Eiffel tower where Bobby took photographs. It was an excellent view from that side of the river. In the afternoon we went downtown to sign transportation papers later visiting the shopping district and had tea at the Café de la Paix.

The Larsens[23] called in the evening and later we took a walk to the Champs Élysées.

---

[23]*Capt. (later Lt. General) and Mrs. Henry Larsen.*

Captain Blake and French WWI monument to the U.S. 2nd Division, Lucy-le-Bocage, 1932.

Saturday we engaged a car to take us to the Battlefield and Belleau Wood. Robert was able to find the exact territory through which he and his company operated. We found the woods where they lay by day and the shell holes and fox holes where they lay at night. It was a hot sultry day. Robert had us walking several miles for about two hours. He showed us where he crossed the wheat field under fire for which he was cited for the D.S.C. and Croix de Guerre. Bobby found three rusty helmets. It hardly seemed possible after these many years have elapsed, but this ground is off the main road several miles. The country was so green that it was difficult to imagine that there had ever been a war there, but Robert said that it had looked green and luxuriant when they were fighting there. The villages have all been restored. Only a few vine-covered ruins remain. We passed over a bridge which had been destroyed three times—in 1817, 1860 and 1917. We regretted that there was not time to visit other battlefields. But we covered the territory near Belleau Wood rather thoroughly. Our chauffeur was an Englishman who had fought in the British Army but had married a French girl and settled in France—

Saturday morning the Larsens took us for a drive to Versailles which was lovely in the sunset light. The Arc de Triomphe is very beautiful lighted up at night. We drove through the Bois de Boulogne and saw some other palaces and the Montmartre and Montparnasse. We stopped at the Cupole where Leontine took us last year. It was a beautiful warm night.

Paris is charming. The taxi drivers were courteous. Everyone was nice to us. I was loathe to leave it.

Early Sunday morning we took the boat train for Le Havre. A few hours later we strolled up the gangway of the *City of Norfolk*. How tiny she looked lying alongside the dock! She was only 14000 tons and not heavily laden. Later in the voyage we had reason to know of her light weight. We sailed at noon. The shores of France grew dim—we were on the Atlantic homeward bound.

Robert Wallace Blake

Chapter 3

Travels 1932 – 1935

After leaving Spain, Rosselet discontinued her travel journal for several years, though her travels did not.

The journey home from Cherbourg was an easy one. Despite initial misgivings about the small size of SS City of Norfolk *we had a smooth ten-day passage in the Gulf Stream to Baltimore. There the family split: Robert to Nicaragua by ship for another term of election duty, Rosselet and Robert W. by train to California to wait for his return. This time with sisters Gladys and Dorothy both married, there was room for both to stay at the parental home in Berkeley, a nice reunion for all.*

In December 1932 Robert's Nicaraguan tour ended and he traveled directly to his next post, at Quantico VA. In January, between school terms, Rosselet and son took the train to San Diego to visit the senior Blakes, then took the Sunset Limited east from Los Angeles to rejoin Robert in Virginia.

For the next two years family travels were limited to day trips and weekends at historic spots in Virginia and Maryland. Then came the orders to join the Navy's Special Service Squadron in the Canal Zone. With another international adventure begun, Rosselet dusted off her travel journal to start a new chapter.

Robert Wallace Blake

Chapter 4

Panama

Panama – January 1936

Last July another foreign tour began. We sailed from New York after two and a half busy and interesting days there, on the *Ancon* for Panama. Leontine was with us. We enjoyed visiting the Metropolitan Art Museum in New York—also a glimpse of Greenwich Village, and New York harbor and Fifth Avenue.

The voyage was uneventful—A short stop of four hours at Port-au-Prince Haiti where we drove to Petionville and spent an hour at the Hotel Splendide with Vee's[24] friend—where we gloried in all the green tropical foliage and the quiet beauty of the white hotel with its large verandas. Away from the Hotel it was warm, humid, smelling of foreign odors. To us it seemed unbearably warm, but there was a breeze while driving. Robert amused us by writing amusing messages to Berk[25] and Bob Smythe[26] in Petionville—There were some fine views of the harbor on the return from Petionville which is up in the hills—Along the way the lovely flamboyant trees in bloom made the drive a picture.

At last on July 10, we arrived in Panama and spent several days at the Tivoli [Hotel] until we could move into an attractive, green house in Vista del Mar.

Blake house in Miramar, Pamama, 1935.

[24]*Mrs. "Dutch" Hermle.*
[25]*Berkeley B. Blake, my father's older brother.*
[26]*An old Berkeley friend.*

Here we have a green lawn, a vine covered fence, with large bell like flowers of blue growing on the vine in masses. It has flowered continually ever since our arrival and is spreading over the entire length of one side of the house. There is a bougainvillea tree at the gate which is now a mass of red blooms. There are hibiscus—red and pink growing on the back fence. We are two blocks from the ocean—A breeze blows almost constantly which is refreshing—we are on a curve in the bay and from the ocean sea wall drive, two blocks away can see the peninsula of Panama opposite us—with its soft colored buildings jutting out into the ocean— the jagged islands and Fort Amador beyond—while Ancon Hill towers above the base of the peninsula.

Panama is a small town made up of narrow winding streets running the length of and crossing the narrow peninsula. It is only a few blocks wide near the Union Club end. One can see the water at either end of the short streets. At the end of the Peninsula is the aforementioned Club which is partially extended out over the rocks and makes a romantic setting for dancing on its terrace at night—especially in the moonlight—Nights in the dry season are heavenly—often in the rainy season they are beautiful but uncertain.

Union Club at night , Panama , 1937.

Also the end of the Peninsula contains a sea wall, part of an ancient fortress used as a prison of which nothing remains but the lower vaults, and the beautiful little Plaza Francia in honor of the French who started the canal. There is a vine-covered walk between the Union Club and Plaza Francia along the sea wall which is very attractive—especially at night. Here we have wandered on several occasions.

The streets of Panama are lined with two story houses of soft pastel colors with overhanging balconies much be-ferned—It is picturesque. The lower floors are occupied by East Indian shops where one can buy everything from the Orient, Italy and Europe—There are a number of Plazas the principal one being the Cathedral Plaza (Independencia) where the City Hall, Post Office, and Hotel Central are located. They all have a green park in the center and are very pretty with palm trees, a central band stand, and walks. Concerts are given Thursday and Sunday evenings.

Empanadas (little crisp meat turnovers) are a special Panamanian dish served at eleven in the morning at the Hotel Central—They are delicious well worth trying as is also *arroz con coco*—and *arroz con pollo*.

The cathedral and churches are interesting but not unusual with the exception of the church of the flat arch which is in ruins but the flat arch has remained these four hundred years since the devout priest finally succeeded in getting it to stand. The story goes that he conceived the idea and built three churches and that each time the arch collapsed but that the each time he prayed and never lost faith in his vision that it could be done as he was doing it in honor of God; though he was laughed to scorn by all. The final time he prayed that if it was not right he would build no more but that if it fell again he asked to be taken with it. When it was completed he himself stood under it and removed the final supporting beam. But it did not fall. It stood. Later the church was burned, but the flat arch stood untouched and has withstood the various earthquakes felt in this tropical city. There is also a church of the Golden Altar—on Avenida B.—which houses the altar which was in the Cathedral in Old Panama during Morgan's raid. The Panamanians whitewashed it so that that pirate would not destroy it. It is covered with gold leaf. Not a particularly outstanding altar—but interesting because of its history connection.

The drive to Old Panama is pleasant through the famous flat *Sabanas* (or prairies). The road passes the Race track and country homes—and finally branches out to the coast about ten miles from Panama. Here stand the ruins of the Old City, the center of the Gold trade of the days of the Spanish galleons. It was one of the richest cities of the world in those colonial days. Morgan utterly destroyed it—Only piles of stone remain—The Cathedral stands in more entirety than the rest—The legend goes that he ordered it destroyed three times and his men in trying to obey were frightened away and that when he attempted to destroy it himself he too was unable to do it because it was surrounded by demons which gave great fright and thereby protected God's abode. They said that it was enchanted. The old walls are covered with vines. Trees grow right out of the stone inside the building—And the vistas of sea, trees and ruins is very picturesque—

Not far away is a native fishing village. It was from such a village that Panama was named for it means "abundant fish." The natives live on fish and rice and a few native root vegetables and fruits such as plantain, bananas, bread fruit papaya, mangos.

The Panama Golf Club is situated on the most beautiful terrain around—high on some hill on the road to Old Panama. From there the view of water, the Panama peninsula, Fort Amador, Taboga Island and on the other side—Old Panama, is enchanting. Here cool breezes blow all day long and even at noon time it is refreshingly cool out here. One may enjoy a delicious luncheon on its shady pleasant veranda, looking out over the sea.

The other very interesting and pleasant drive is out through Pedro Miguel, past the Canal and locks through a native jungle preserve to the Madden Dam. The jungle is cool green refreshing about four o'clock after the heat of the day.

So we have spent six months in the tropics—It is far more liveable than the East coast in summer. Never does one experience the sultry enervating heat of a Washington or Virginia summer day and night. We have a constant breeze—It is always beautiful at night and in the early morning, in fact often it is cold at night—We have adjusted ourselves very easily and thoroughly enjoy the climate.

Our life as naval officers families has been pleasant. We have had an agreeable social life meeting and mixing with those attached to the Special Service Squadron, the 15th Naval District and meeting some from the various Army Posts, and officials of the Panama Canal and some from Panama and the diplomatic circles.

As we do not care to make our lives a continuous round of social affairs we have not called at any of the Legations excepting the United States, and one or two of the Central American countries. We met these ministers at the Admiral's various receptions and official dinners and, liking to talk Spanish, Robert was desirous of knowing as many people who speak the Castilian tongue as possible. We were pleased to make the acquaintance of the Mexican Minister and Mrs Padilla. They lived next door to us in Spain on Calle de Velázquez in Madrid for several months. Mrs Padilla remembered us, tho' we never met, as she was a lovely bride then, from Norfolk Virginia, and remembered hearing that some American officers and their families were living in the apartment.

Vice Admiral Best and the officers of H.M.S. *York* were here early in January and we were caught in a round of social offers which had begun during the Christmas holidays—the British Minister and Miss Adam introduced them at a large reception at the Legation—then there was a Governor's dinner at the Tivoli and several receptions to which we were invited acting as host at one. We met some of them informally at the Union club one evening and found them very friendly approachable and likeable young chaps.

Special Service Squadron duty is spent part of the time cruising, part of the time in port. From July to the middle of September they made a cruise of Caribbean ports—Cartagena—Jamaica, Barbados, Curaçao, Virgin Islands, Cuba, a port in Mexico, Honduras and Swan Islands. It proved very interesting with much entertaining and pleasant swimming at country clubs, and fishing and hunting. It was a "Good Will" cruise.

At present they are away at Culebra taking part in the Fleet Marine Force maneuvers and will return in a month.

We are not so lonely as during the first cruise. Of course at that time the ships left after we had been here only one week. We had not become adjusted and knew no-one. This time we have a large circle of friends—though a number of our best friends have departed with the departure of the *Trenton*. Our husbands have been transferred to the *Memphis*,[27] the new flagship of the Squadron, changing with the Admiral and his staff. We were sorry to bid goodbye to the Folzs and the Richmonds. But sometime surely we shall meet again—One does at last, in the Navy.

---

[27] *U.S.S.* Memphis *brought Lindbergh home from France after his historic 1927 flight.*

Chapter 5

Travels 1937 – 1940

From Panama, the Blake family moved to Washington DC in the summer of 1937. Robert was detached from the Special Service Squadron in Havana after interviewing then President Batista. He took leave to visit his parents in Southern California. He had not seen them in four years. Rosselet and son Robert Wallace took the Dollar liner SS President Harding *from Balboa to Long Beach, where Robert met them. After visiting the senior Blakes in Spring Valley and the Wallaces in Los Altos, the family drove across the country in their 1933 Dodge, un-air-conditioned in those days. They made brief scenic stops at Lake Tahoe, Yellowstone National Park, and Jackson Lake. In Chicago they visited with Blake brother Garnet and his family, newly returned from years in Chile, and also met Blake brother Berkeley and his family, returning to California from a visit to the east coast.*

In Washington, Robert and Rosselet found a newly-built house for rent across the Potomac in Arlington, then sent their son off to college in Cambridge. As was the custom in those days, he went by himself.

After a year in Arlington, the Blakes moved to an older house in Washington itself, across the street from the Adolf Berle estate on Cathedral Avenue. There they remained for the rest of Robert's tour at the Navy Building. In the spring of 1939 Robert was assigned temporary duty with the Seventh Cruiser Division— Flag Secretary to Admiral Husband Kimmel for a Goodwill Cruise around South America. Wives were not invited.

In the summer of 1940, newly promoted to Colonel, Robert was ordered to take the Senior Course at the Navy War College in a class that included Colonel (later Lt. General) Roy Geiger. Robert and Rosselet drove to Newport in their new DeSoto. They settled in one-half of a duplex saltbox house on Cranston Avenue.

With a son away in college, and friends yet to be made, Rosselet took up her neglected travel journal and started a new chapter.

Chapter 6

Returning Home

Newport, Rhode Island   **August 26, 1940**

The desire to keep record of our tour at Panama lagged—and so there is no note made of our last year and a half there. They were busy pleasant months on the whole. New many and Central American friends—pleasant outing to Taboga Island where we had steak suppers and swimming parties—going over in Navy motor sailors or launches; trips into the interior, such as La Venta where we enjoyed the beautiful white coral sand beach and the excellent little Inn and delicious food, trips across the Canal where the ships sailed from Colón for a cruise and we spent the night there at the Hotel—gay happy evenings at the Union Club and Beer Gardens where the officers and wives from the *Memphis* had jolly parties while the ships were in with the Meyers and Williams as Admiral.

Here too Bob spent his last two years in High School and had a teacher,[28] a graduate and MA from MIT who caused Bob's interest in an engineering course to bud. Here Bob was appointed to be Editor of his School magazine *Zonian* and spent many hours in his last six months working on it mounting photographs and writing articles and trying to get others to do their work. This was a real problem for he spent so much time on it that for several weeks he hardly had any sleep. But at last it was done and Commencement came. Robert was away—so I heard him practice his commencement address. He was the top man in his class but there was no Valedictorian because neither he nor the next highest student, an army officer's daughter, had been in the school for over two years. So the five top students were noted as Honor Students and each one made an address. It was a very proud and happy parent who attended the Commencement Exercises and looked in on the Senior Dance. He spoke extraordinarily well—it seemed to me, and others spoke of it. My only regret was that his father was not present. What a dear boy he has been! He has never given us a worry nor an anxious moment as result of his conduct or school work. He is extremely companionable and a good friend as well as a son. He was able to enter MIT without an examination because he stood in the upper tenth of his class—a general rule for accredited High School Students—and he got an Army and Navy scholarship which pays half his tuition fee. Which he has continued to receive every year for his four years there.

---

[28] *Edward M. Pease. He had a BS from Purdue and an ScD from MIT.*

From 1937 to 1940 we were in Washington D.C. where Robert continued his Latin contacts, with the Attachés of the Latin American Embassies. He was in the Office of Naval Intelligence having the Latin American desk and made many good friends during our three years there. When we left, the Attachés gave him a handsome silver cigarette box with their names all engraved on it. And we were genuinely sad to leave such good friends as the Léon-Gomez from Columbia, the Cortis from Chile, the Zermeños from Mexico, the Berzunzas, the Godoys, the Arraujos from Brazil, and several others. As well as having to part before that with the Rugas from Chile, and the [   ] from Argentina.

Robert made a goodwill cruise of South America in the spring of 1939 on the *San Francisco* as Admiral Kimmel's aide—really as Spanish interpreter—They visited all South American capitals and went through the Straits. I remained in Washington alone—and made a short trip to Boston in June—a visit to the General Meeting of the Mother Church—and saw Bob every evening. He was attending summer session—a required course in Shop work. We had dinner together and some pleasant drives and dinners with the Holcombs[29] who drove us out to Plymouth and about Boston. Also visited the Chestnut Hill home of Mrs Eddy and the Benevolent Association and Publishing Society.

Now the three years in Washington are finished—We found it interesting—hard work for Robert—and rather gay socially as we had not only the Latin Attachés but our Marine and Navy friends—also a few civilians. Clara Safford an old family friend and her mother[30] were very kind and we saw a good deal of them. Gladys Partridge Domeratsky a Berkeley family friend whose husband Louis (a Russian) is in the Department of Commerce we saw now and again—They have a place in the country at McLean. Naomi Alexander, a friend from my government working days in Washington 1919-20 at 1336 Harvard St.; had a luncheon at her house in Bethesda which I enjoyed and she came to one I gave at the Olney Inn. Also saw Kathleen Smith and her husband.

We had many of our oldest friends in the Marine Corps at Quantico our first two years in Washington, but the whole crowd went to San Diego the last year. And had visits from friends passing through and from the family.

So we sweltered in the summer but enjoyed the rest of the year—and the social and official life—with two Army and Navy Receptions at the White House and many parties at the Embassies. Now at last we have spent a beautiful cool summer in New England—going often to the beach and taking the lovely walks and drives about Newport. Robert is at the Naval War College here taking the course which

[29] *Friends of my grandparents*
[30]*Mrs. Safford was 106 years old in 1938. Her father was the first director of the Smithsonian.*

is normally an eleven month's course. It is all rigged to give the meat of it in four months which will be by the first of November, on account of the War.

The beautiful countries of France and Spain have been war ridden since we visited there. The Spanish Civil War with its defeat of liberalism and return to power of the old vested interests of church and aristocracy seemed very sad to us. Having known some of the intellectuals of the Republic and having taken an interest in its welfare it seemed sad that the church and ruling wealthy families should get back the power. For they have kept Spain a retarded country for so many years.

Newport is a beautiful sleepy little town; covered with handsome trees and magnificent estates. It is on the island section of Rhode Island. It has a number of old historic landmarks—houses and other places marked by important events in the Revolutionary War. We are getting around to them one by one.

We enjoy the fine Cliff walk which follows the coast line for three and a half miles past the gardens of many of the handomest estates so that one has a view of the lovely gardens and expanses of lawn, the great mansions and superb views of the Sea. Every Tuesday afternoon during the summer there is a garden tour to one or two of the estates where we get a more minute view of some of the most superb gardens in the country. Tomorrow we make our last tour as the season ends in August and we see the John Jacob Astor gardens of Chetwode and the Berwind estate "The Elms"—We have seen many others—the "Blue Garden," "Rose Garden," "Swiss Village" of the author Curtis James, the Auchincloss Farm, the Alexander Hamilton Rice estate, the estate of the Van Burens, "Gray Craig," are among those that stand out as well as "The Breakers," the Vanderbilt Estate.

Newport has many fine beaches—Baileys Beach being the fashionable one. But the Navy crowd go to a small beach club at Third Beach run by Mrs Van Buren. Here the water is quiet—there is no surf excepting after a storm. It makes in-shore swimming fine and the water is fairly warm. We have spent much of our time at Third Beach; but the season is short and the cool days last week made us realize that fall is coming. There will doubtless be little swimming until next summer.

Already we have experienced a New England Clam-bake—a most elaborate affair. There are professional clam bakers who come to prepare it in proper fashion. They prepare a fire and a bed of hot stones and then put on the fish, potatoes, corn, sausages, brown bread all wrapped in paper—and the clams and lobsters, them put on a special kind of sea-weed containing much water in the little balls on it, and then a wet canvass over all. A clam chowder is prepared in another cauldron—and a green salad, watermelon and coffee served with the meal. It's delicious—I did not care for the brown bread flavored with sea weed but liked all else. The Navy had the Clam Bake at Coddington Point. Bob had just returned from Engineering ROTC in Virginia so he accompanied us. We had only been in Newport a few weeks we did not know many people here but enjoyed the Clambake and met some very pleasant new people, the Basslers—the Moores, the McKittricks & the McCalls.

Another pastime in Newport is Antiquing—visiting auctions and antique shops. Have already found some decanters—are now looking for andirons.

Social life is pleasant but fairly quiet in the summer. Everyone goes to the beach as much as possible. We have attended about one party a week since we came, occasionally two. This is a real rest after Washington. But with the garden tours Tuesdays and summer plays Friday evenings and one or two parties and swimming almost every day we have kept pleasantly occupied. Bob comes home from his summer course at MIT every week end. He is taking some lab courses to ease his work during the year.

We made a trip to Boston yesterday visiting "Ye Olde Blake House" in Dorchester built in 1650—a brother of the Vermont and New Hampshire Blakes from which Robert's father came.[31] We hope to make a trip to New Hampshire and Vermont next week end visiting Sharon and South Royalton where there are cousins and the old grandfather's home in Hill, New Hampshire.

We drove about the old part of Boston, seeing the Old North Church, King's Chapel, the Old South Meeting House, Faneuil Hall, Beacon Hill, Bunker Hill, the Boston Common, etc. Also drove out to beautiful Wellesley College.—And to the Airport. Bob was our guide. And we visited Harvard University and Cambridge and had dinner at the Coach House Inn, the home of Longfellow's Village Blacksmith.

Not long ago we all attended a Garden Party for British war relief at Harbor Court, the Nicholson estate. The Honorable Nadine Stoner, daughter of Lord and Lady C_____ was in charge. She is dark and wore a bright watermelon pink tea gown which was auctioned off. Her sister and many young girls from the summer colony were there. The Sokes girl and a number of others modelled gowns in a Fashion Show. The daughter of Lord and Lady Mountbatten sold us a British pin—a most attractive girl. About four thousand dollars was made.

Some time I shall tell you about the Art Association.

This was the last entry in my mother's journal. We shall never learn about the Art Association.

---

[31] *We learned later the families were unrelated.*

Epilog

Last Travels

In May 1941 Col. and Mrs. Blake moved from Newport RI to Quantico VA to join the 5th Regiment. Later in the summer the regiment moved to New River NC where there were as yet no family quarters, so Rosselet Blake took an apartment in New York to be with her son, then working for Pan American Airways. On December 7, 1941, they were both at dinner with old Navy friends from Panama and Newport.

After Pearl Harbor there was a new job for the 5th Regiment and a new assignment for Colonel Blake. Rosselet joined her husband for the long drive across the country to join his new command in San Diego, where he would be organizing and training a new Defense Battalion. While the battalion was organizing, Rosselet and Robert found a Spanish-style house to rent in La Jolla much like the house they had dreamed of in Toledo nine years earlier.

Blake house at 6011 Ocean Drive, La Jolla, 1942.

In August 1942 Colonel Blake and the 10th Defense Battalion shipped out from San Diego to join the war in the Pacific. Rosselet knew that her husband would return safely one day, but she knew not when, so she left La Jolla to wait for him in Berkeley, where they first had met, and where family, friends, and the church of her childhood still abided.

Rosselet in her garden, Berkeley, 1944.

In Berkeley, Rosselet took a garden apartment at 1545 Scenic Avenue just a few blocks from her former Arch Street home. As she waited, Robert and his Marines traveled, island by island, from Oahu to Florida Is, to the Russells, Guadalcanal, and Bougainville. On July 1, 1944, Robert was at sea, preparing to land with the 3rd Marine Division on the beach at the Japanese stronghold of Guam. General Lem Shepherd, commanding the landing, had to break the news to his comrade from Belleau Woods of 1918, that Rosselet Blake had died in her sleep the previous night.

Robert Blake did indeed return safely from World War II, as a Brigadier General. From 1946 to 1949 he traveled the world as Inspector General of the Marine Corps, inspecting Marine Corps installations, but he traveled alone. He retired in 1949 as a Major General and continued to travel. He revisited Spain, France, Panama, and Mexico, but not with Rosselet. He did not rejoin Rosselet until 1983, when he died at Lake Park Retirement Residence, in Oakland CA.

Today Rosselet and Robert are interred together in Golden Gate National Cemetery in San Bruno CA.

the end

Rosselet Blake, Los Altos, CA 1943

About the Author

Robert Wallace Blake was born in Quantico, Virginia, and grew up as Marine Corps dependent on and off posts, in the U.S.A., Spain and Panama. He graduated from the M.I.T. and was a Naval Aviator during World War II.

Mr. Blake had a forty-year career with Pan American Airways based in New York and Seattle, plus overseas assignments in Afghanistan, Africa and France. He has written a number of articles in technical, military and historical journals, book reviews and Op Ed pieces for Seattle newspapers.

Mr. Blake's most recent book is *Bayonets and Bougainvilleas*, 1st Books Library, 2001.

On the Cover

The red-and-gold shield with centered caltrap is the insignia of the 3rd Marine Division which fought at Bougainville in World War II.

The star-and-Indianhead symbol is the insignia of the 2nd Infantry Division in which the Marine Brigade fought at Belleau Wood in World War I.

Printed in the United States
23317LVS00006B/463-486